Everywhere
The River Goes

Bill Buckley

*All photos by Bill Buckley kayaking the Waters of Mississippi.
 Cover photo is the Mighty Mississippi River near Natchez.

**The illustrations and stories in this book are from real life experiences unless stated otherwise.

ISBN: 9798366643887

 Published by: YesBear Publishing
info@YesBearPublishing.com

TABLE OF CONTENTS

Preface

Putting words on paper helps me to process who I believe God and myself to be. I seek freedom from trying to accomplish spirituality through my obedience to laws and empty traditions. I need to know the clear, bold truth of Christ and what His presence means. Given the chance, I hope that I would love you well but it may not look like Southern culture, American culture, or Church culture.

I need for you to believe with me for a breakthrough in my life and maybe even yours. If one of these messages helps you to better know God, His love and purpose, it would have been worth the work. This book is not about helping you to spend "quality time" with God every day. He is not one of many things we are attempting to fit into our busy lives. We need to spend all our time connecting with God every day! That is not an unreasonable burden. It is the only response of a desperate heart. I've got to have what is only found in Him, that which is real and pure and beautiful! It's work unless you know Him, then it's amazingly abundant life!

Bill Buckley
2022

ADVERSITY

"Consider it pure joy, my brothers and sisters, whenever you face trials of many kinds, because you know that the testing of your faith produces perseverance. Let perseverance finish its work so that you may be mature and complete, not lacking anything." (James 1:2-4)

Gulf of Mexico

If God was a Good God

For years I've been buying running shoes at discount stores, but I recently visited a genuine sports shoe store that sells nothing but running shoes and gear. They measured me by having me stand on this high-tech imaging machine that captured the exact size and structure of my feet. Next, they matched me with the perfect shoe. As I switched from exercising in my old shoes to the new, my legs began to hurt. What I discovered was that the old shoes were not supporting me effectively. When the new shoes made proper adjustments in my muscles and joints, the immediate result was pain.

It's like that with Jesus. When we've been living with a cheap version of the truth and then start walking in the beauty of Christ, the immediate effect is usually pain. We start realizing how broken we really were. The correction the Lord brings to our lives hurts, not because He is mean, but because we were so out of alignment. I'm going to go further and be healthier with these new shoes, the same thing that happened when I "put on" Christ! In the process pain is inevitable but so is victory!

Two common "alignment issues" when someone begins their walk with God:

False identity.

Being new in Christ means new to the core of who you are! Learning to run the race from your new identity means walking away from any behaviors, attitudes, or beliefs that ruled your old life. "That, in reference to your former manner of life, you lay aside the old self, which is being corrupted in accordance with the lusts of deceit, and that you be renewed in the spirit of your mind, and put on the new self, which in the likeness of God has been created in righteousness and holiness of the truth." (Ephesians 4:22-24)

False view of God.

Only the Holy Spirit can give true revelation about the nature and heart of God. The Good News is that when you receive Christ, the Spirit will guide you into all the truth. He will not speak on His own authority, but whatever He hears He will speak. It's comforting and exciting to know that God is active in the lives of those who love Him!

Walking With a Limp

When I was a rookie trying to make the New York Jets football team, I tore a hamstring muscle. At the time, I had much compromise in my life and I was not taking care of myself on a level that the NFL demands. Because I could not get back to full speed in time, I was cut from the team. I came home to Mississippi with my tail between my legs. I still favor that right leg. I still walk with a limp.

Jacob, one of the fathers of the Christian faith, also had a limp. He found himself between a rock and a hard place when he failed to follow God's orders and cheated his brother Esau out of valuable livestock. When Esau discovered what Jacob had done, he summoned his army of 400 fighters and went after him! Jacob was getting squeezed between God's will and an enemy's anger!

One night when Jacob was alone on the edge of nowhere, a mighty angel of God showed up in his camp. The Bible says that they wrestled all night until the Angel touched Jacob's leg and dislocated it! After that encounter Jacob began to discover his true purpose. But for the rest of his life, he walked with a limp as a reminder of that holy encounter. (See Genesis 32)

If I'm going to follow Jesus, it's going to be with a limp. He allows us to get broken so we can acknowledge our weakness and learn to follow Him! Don't try to outrun your limp. It's a reminder of God's love for you! His message to us—"My grace is sufficient for you, for my power is made perfect in your weakness." (2 Corinthians 12:9)

He Found Us

I got cut from the New York Jets Football team when I was a 21-year-old rookie. The next day I got a call from the New England Patriots who wanted me to sign as a free agent. That drive from Hempstead, Long Island to Foxboro, Massachusetts was the longest drive of my life. Halfway there I pulled off the road and called the Patriots head coach. It was a short conversation. I said, "Coach, I'm not coming." He said, "OK Bill. Good luck."

And with that the most prolific period of my young life was over. I pointed our car south and Mary and I drove toward nowhere. In the next 5 years I had 5 different jobs and we lived in 4 different places. It was a raw time in our lives and marriage. Little did I know that we were being tracked by the Hound of Heaven.

I had no place in my life for God, but in His great love, He made a place. Looking back, we can see how He was speaking to us in those hard times. Maybe our encounters with Him can help you if you are in the middle of struggle.

God exploited our adversity in very elementary ways. In those days when my head hit the pillow at night, I would often think of Him. Looking back I can see He was drawing me in those late night moments. He inspired key people to intercept our lives with truth, some who were hard and some who were tender. He honored our rookie attempts at trying to understand the Bible. Finally, He led us to a group of Christians who loved us through our immaturity and led us to consistency. He's so good!

No Free Lunch

When baby eagles get to a certain size, everything changes! One day the mother eagle comes back from hunting, but this time there's no food in her beak and she doesn't land on the edge of the nest. Instead, she hovers about three feet over the nest like a hummingbird. She is demonstrating that those curious appendages on her babies' backs have a useful function.

Eagles were meant to fly, but when they are young they don't know that yet. If we take an eagle and separate it at birth from its parents, it will never learn to fly. It will just awkwardly stumble around in the dirt like a chicken. All at once the mother eagle pushes the young one out of the nest and it falls down the face of the cliff. In a flash the great mother flies down, catches the little one on her back and flies up to deposit it back in the nest.

It all looks like a terrible, unnecessary experience for the young eagles. But the very thing that seems abusive is the same thing that creates in the eaglets the will to fly! Do you ever feel like somebody pushed you over the edge? Your life is a free-fall and nobody seems to know it but you. Don't forget this great truth—When the food stops, God gives the grace to fly!

"Do not gloat over me, my enemies! For though I fall, I will rise again. Though I sit in darkness, the LORD will be my light." (Micah 7:8) "For you God have been my help, and in the shadow of your wings I will sing for joy. My soul clings to you; your right hand upholds me." (Ps. 63:7-8)

God is not holding out on you. He's holding on to you!

Street Corner Faith

I know a guy who was born into a messed up, dysfunctional family. He basically raised himself and seemed destined to the same desperate poverty. Still just a teenager, he attended a revival meeting with thousands of other people and gave his life to the Jesus Christ. He had no Christian or church experience whatsoever. All He had was a desperate, hungry heart and the Holy Spirit.

One of the first things he ever did as a new Christian was to stand on the street corner of his city every Saturday morning. He tried to tell everyone who came by him about Jesus Christ and his new life. A tall, skinny teenager on a street corner in New York. It's what he could do.

If you follow the Lord, sooner or later you are not going to look normal. Allowing people to take advantage of you for some purpose of God might look foolish to others. Giving to someone who is not responsible enough to wisely steward your gift makes you look gullible. The Pharisees really thought that Jesus was weak because he could not even save Himself.

Who will you look like today? Pause this morning and ask God to move your heart for those who are lost and hurting. Be willing to step out of your comfort zone and do something for them. By the way, that skinny kid sharing his faith on the street corner? His name is Mike Cavanaugh and in the last 30 years God has used him in astonishing ways as a nationally recognized evangelist, Bible school president, and leader of leaders. Small start. Big influence. Faithfulness is not giving something big. It's giving what you have. "As each one has received a special gift, employ it in serving one another as good stewards of the manifold grace of God." (I Peter 4:10)

Response Time

What coaches tell athletes is true for you and me—If you get in the game long enough, you're going to make a mistake. A fumble, a dropped pass, an interception, a missed tackle or missed block, maybe a missed field goal. Nobody plays the perfect game. Most likely the mistake is not what will get us beat. It's your response to the mistake that gets us beat.

Responses like frustration, embarrassment, blaming a teammate or coach—reactions that shut you down and take you out of the game. If we are going to win, we got to avoid these momentum-killing responses. When you make a mistake, remember who you are. Stay true to your identity and don't let a mistake define you. Remember who we are and don't let mistakes destroy unity with your coaches and teammates.

If a teammate makes a mistake, go get him back in the game. Prepare your mind for action. Get your head right and stay focused on the big picture. Most of all, set your heart by showing up prayed up. Remember, there's only one who never made a mistake, the One who died for your mistakes—Jesus Christ, the original Champion! "Brothers, there's one thing that will give us victory, forgetting what lies behind and straining forward to what lies ahead, we press on toward the goal to win the prize laid out before us both here on earth and in heaven." (Philippians 4:13-14)

God and Tragedies

The plane crash that killed the Marshall University football team occurred on Nov. 14, 1970. Every one of the 75 people on board died in the crash, including the coaches. The tragedy shocked the town of Huntington, WV in the worst way imaginable. Dozens of families were forced to mourn the deaths of their sons, husbands, and fathers that sad day. The crash is still considered the worst air disaster in American sports history and holds a sobering place in my own heart.

That particular Southern Airways plane was scheduled to drop off the Marshall Team and then fly to Baton Rouge to pick up our Mississippi State Team of which I was a member. If that plane had held together only a matter of hours longer, it could have been the MS State players and coaches who died.

This sad story holds some significant theological implications. I've had Christian people tell me that my team lived because fate was with us and not with the Marshall team. Fate is usually thought of as a predetermined course of events beyond human control. A typical response to a belief in fate is resignation—if we can't change destiny, then why even try? Whatever happens, happens, and we can't do anything about it. This is called "fatalism," and it is not biblical.

The Bible teaches that Man was created with the ability to make moral choices and that he is responsible for those choices. The Fall of Man was not a predetermined event in which Adam and Eve were hapless victims of a Puppet-Master God. On the contrary, Adam and his wife had been given full authority to choose obedience (with its attendant blessing) or disobedience (with its consequent curse). They knew what the result of their decision would be, and they were held accountable (Genesis 3).

Because of their original choices, bad things now happen on earth, like young football players dying in a plane crash before their lives even get started. What happens to us on earth may be out of our control. But our response to anything that happens to us is 100% in our control. Tragedies became a proving ground for some of the world's greatest saints! With God's guidance, we can change our destiny through our obedient choices.

Diagnostic Charge

I was at an auto repair shop where a man was loudly complaining about the diagnostic charge—the cost of finding out what's wrong with your car. He complained, "You want to charge me for just looking at my engine and you haven't even fixed the problem!" He walked out of the place and drove off in his still-broken vehicle.

What people don't realize is that it costs time and experience to go into an engine and figure out what's preventing it from running effectively. Do we expect our mechanics to do that for free? I wonder if sometimes we don't treat the Lord like this guy treated his mechanic.

Your life isn't running right so you go to the Him in prayer asking Him to fix it. Then He says, "I will gladly do that but it's going to cost you. You're going to have to stop making excuses for yourself. You're going to have to quit being defensive when I use other people to point out weaknesses in you that keep you from loving and serving me and others. You're going to have to confess that sin in your life that only you and I know about."

And like this guy with the broken Chevy, we walk out on God and limp along the highway of life offended and still broken. Salvation is free but that diagnostic charge will cost you! Go ahead and pay it with honesty and humility remembering God's beautiful promise to you—

"So do not fear, for I am with you; do not be dismayed, for I am your God. I will strengthen you and help you; I will uphold you with my righteous right hand." (Isaiah 41:10)

Homeless

I'm drawn to homeless people because I'm so much like them. In college, I tried to find a home on a football team and in a fraternity, but I really didn't fit either place. I wanted to be a counter-culture hippie but all I got was a gypsy life. After college, I tried to be a businessman and then a pastor but soon I was back out on the "Street to Nowhere" trying to find something that would feed my heart.

These days I have a recurring daydream that often happens in the pauses of my life. It's a moment in time when I see a lonely road ahead leading only to death. I can identify with Solomon of the Bible who proclaimed, "I have looked on all my works that my hands have done, and on the labor that I have labored to do and look! The whole is vanity and confusion, and there is no advantage under the sun!" (Ecclesiastes 2:11)

Sounds like a homeless man to me. Don't misunderstand me. My life is full of meaning and purpose. I'm not an unhappy person, I just don't belong here. I'm not home yet and, until then, I'm working to take every person I can to the forever-house of the Lord!

"The Lord GOD says, 'Behold, I am laying in Zion a stone, a tested stone, a costly cornerstone for the foundation, firmly placed. He who believes in it will not be disturbed'." (Isaiah

28:16) Now that's the house I'm looking for! Can't wait to hear the Lord say, "Welcome home, Bill!"

Pain and Gain

When I was coaching high school basketball we lost in triple overtime to our biggest rival. Our kids played so hard that it broke my heart to look at their faces as we huddled at our bench. We were all crushed. At the time, none of us knew that would become our defining moment. Those kids could have folded and coasted for the rest of the season. They didn't! We went on to become conference champions, finishing with the best record in school history!

The pain of that triple overtime loss forged something in our hearts. A powerful conviction rose up in those guys from the suffering of defeat. I'm reminded of Jesus and His defining moment. The Scriptures tell us, "When the days were approaching for Jesus to be crucified and to be risen from the dead, He set His face to go to Jerusalem." (Luke 9:51, my emphasis) Sold out. That's what happened. Being sold out to the Father's will carries us safely through all defeat and, sooner or later leads to victory! Set your face to go all the way! If you will not give in, hardship will reveal the overcomer in you!

When you get beat, here are some great things to remember: The Lord is for you so who can defeat you? (Psalm 27:1) "Blessed is a man who perseveres under trial; for once he has been approved, he will receive the crown of life which the Lord has promised to those who love Him." (James 1:12) Translation—We never quit!

Wind Health

The biosphere is the space on the Earth's surface where land, air, and water interact with each other to support life. It ranges from heights of up to 41,000 ft. above sea level to depths of at least 26,000 ft. in the ocean. The biosphere marks the range of life on our planet.

Several years ago, scientists built a biosphere in Arizona. The idea was to create a clean, protected environment in which they planted all sorts of beautiful plants and trees. The setting was clean, but it was not healthy. Eventually the limbs of the trees began to break. The trees did not have the benefit of storm winds which cause tree limbs to gain strength!

As a servant of Jesus Christ, I often find myself praying that God will deliver me from my problems, pain, and suffering. Honestly, I want a life where everything is going my way. But that's nothing but a fake biosphere. The strength in us today is a result of God allowing us to experience the winds of adversity yesterday! Living in the middle of God's plan for our lives always gives our pain a purpose! If our eyes are on Him, we can rejoice at those storm clouds coming! The Lord "comforts us in our troubles so that we can comfort others." (2 Cor. 1:4)

Some encouraging words form the Lord about adversity: "If you faint in the day of trouble, your strength is small!" (Pro.24:10) "In every way we're troubled, but we aren't crushed by our troubles. We're frustrated, but we don't give up. We're persecuted, but we're not abandoned. We're captured, but we're not killed. We always carry around the death of Jesus in our bodies so that the life of Jesus is also shown in our bodies." (2 Corinthians 4:8-10) "I leave you peace; my peace I give you." I do not give it to you as the world does. So don't let your hearts be troubled or afraid." (John 14:27)

Abandoned

When he was 5 years old, Bill Wilson's mom took him to a bus stop and told him to wait there until she returned. He waited all day, but she never came back. She had abandoned him forever. For the next several years little Bill moved from one orphanage or foster home to another.

Until one year he landed in the home of a Christian couple who began to take him to church. One Sunday morning he gave His life to Jesus Christ.

As Bill grew up, his passion and faith in Christ increased. As a young adult he founded what would become the largest youth ministry in New York City's history. The ministry took in kids just like Bill who had been abandoned and lost in the system. In the following years, thousands of parentless children found an education, a family, and the Lord through Bill's ministry.

We are all born abandoned to our sin and separated from our Father God. The heartbreak and brokenness of our lives will get progressively worse or powerfully transformed. Are you living under the spell of your own unforgiveness, angry at those who abandoned you?

No matter what your age, you can come home to God and let Him heal you! I pray that you don't come short of the His grace made available for your adoption into the Family of God. (Hebrews 12:15) Take heart! The Lord longs to redeem your pain and restore your life! If you've already been rescued by the Lord, can you see a "Bill Wilson" anywhere in your life? Follow Jesus and help them. He's already on the scene working to win their heart because He is "the Father of the fatherless"! (Psalm 68:5)

He Gets Us Ready

If my parents and their generation of adults were parenting today, I wonder if our current culture would not label them as neglectful, mean, and even abusive. They taught us to take risks and do dangerous things. I owned a gun and hunted alone before I was 10 years old. Before I had a driver's license, I drove all kinds of farm equipment and camped alone in the deep woods without adults building fires and exploring the 250 acres we lived on.

My brothers and I bought and raised our own cattle and sheep for profit. We were responsible for feeding and grooming thousand-pound steers! We learned that you either made money or went broke. We could not leave the table without eating everything on our plates. We got spanked often. In high school I was once grounded for 4 months!

But through all those hard learning years we were never once abandoned nor neglected. My Dad and Mom didn't set us up to fail. They set us up to grow! They came alongside us, preparing us for the dangers, challenges, and responsibilities of life. I'm far from perfect but I think they did a great job preparing me to be a responsible adult.

Most importantly, my brothers and I came to believe in their love and devotion for us. We learned to trust them. My parents were modeling what our relationship with God should be like. He expects a lot from us, but He doesn't leave us on our own to get it figured out or fail. When our hearts are open, He will train us, equip us, and walk with us. Where was the Lord when Shadrach, Meshach, and Abednego got thrown into the fiery furnace? He was in the fiery furnace! (Daniel 3) "Consider it pure joy my brothers and sisters, whenever you face trials of many kinds..." (James 1:2-4) God is neither neglectful nor indifferent. He's beside you! He's getting you ready!

He is Light

One of the most remarkable places I've ever visited is Carlsbad Caverns in the Guadalupe Mountains of New Mexico. This national park covers 73 sq. miles! When we got a couple miles deep into the cave, our tour guide asked all of us to turn off our flashlights and headlamps. We were not prepared for what happened next.

The darkness was so complete that you literally could not see your hand in front of your face! Even after your eyes had a minute to adjust! No light. No shadows. Nothing. Most of us in that group later confessed that fear came on us in a new way. I will never forget that moment and often think about it as I live in the marvelous light of Jesus! As we follow Christ, one day all darkness will be gone from our lives! Here are some extraordinary things the Bible says about light:

God doesn't promise us a life free of darkness. He promises us that if we are with Him, we can safely navigate all darkness. (Psalm 18:28; John 8:12)

When we pursue God, revelation light will grow in us exponentially! (Ps. 97:11; 119:130)

In Christ, we ARE light! (Ephesians 5:8)

Our calling is to live not only in God's light but FROM God's light. The one gives you peace, the other helps you give your peace to others. I Peter 2:9; Eph. 5:8)

If you are feeling overwhelmed or depressed, give yourself to the hungry and help the afflicted and your light will rise in the darkness and your gloom will become like midday! (Isaiah 58:10)

Soon the Light will extinguish all darkness forever! (Luke 8:17; Rev. 22:5)

Confidence

Decades ago, before the LSU baseball team became a dominant national power, they found themselves in the SEC championship game. One more out and they would be

SEC Champs for the first time ever. With two men on base and two outs in the bottom of the ninth, the batter hit an easy fly ball to LSU's right fielder. He dropped it. LSU lost and it was years later before they began to be consistent winners. When asked later about what should have been an easy out, the right fielder made a staggering comment—"I knew my teammates didn't believe I would catch it. I knew I would drop it."

Something was missing from that team. They had talent, coaching, and opportunity but they didn't believe in one another yet. There is a respect that must be earned through dedication and ability. But there is another kind of respect that believes in and honors others, no matter what. It's not conditional. It's not based on how good you are or how well you played. It's a gift. The Message Bible says, "God will never give up on you. Never forget that." (I Corinthians 1:8). When I am confident in God's unconditional respect for me, I get released to reach my greatest potential. Failure becomes opportunity. Weakness gets covered by His power and grace. Somebody needs you to believe in them today, no matter what!

"Do you see someone skilled in their work? They will serve before kings; they will not serve before officials of low rank." (Proverb 22:29)

"For we are God's handiwork, created in Christ Jesus to do good works, which God prepared in advance for us to do." (Ephesians 2:10)

"Each of you should use whatever gift you have received to serve others, as faithful stewards of God's grace in its various forms. If anyone speaks, they should do so as one who speaks the very words of God. If anyone serves, they should do so with the strength God provides, so that in all things God may be praised through Jesus Christ. To him be the glory and the power for ever and ever. Amen." (I Peter 4:10-11)

APOLOGETICS

"But even if you should suffer for the sake of righteousness, you are blessed. AND DO NOT FEAR THEIR INTIMIDATION, AND DO NOT BE TROUBLED, but sanctify Christ as Lord in your hearts, always being ready to make a defense to everyone who asks you to give an account for the hope that is in you, yet with gentleness and reverence." (I Peter 3:14-15)

The Mississippi River

Wilderness Whisper

I camped in some of the deepest woods in Mississippi where I didn't hear human or man-made sounds for four days. Just me and nature. I took day-long hikes and the longer I was there, the closer I felt to the Creator. After the sounds of civilization had been quieted in my soul, it was as if the woods were straining to tell me something.

Before you dismiss me as a strange "tree hugger" as some people call it, you should read Psalm 148 and multiple other Bible verses that speak of creation revealing the glory and presence of God. Sometimes we dismiss people who have a special sensitivity to nature. But God's word is very clear— all of the natural world speaks boldly of his greatness! We worship Him but respect nature. Job put it beautifully—

"But ask the animals, and they will teach you, or the birds in the sky, and they will tell you; or speak to the earth, and it will teach you, or let the fish in the sea inform you. Which of all these does not know that the hand of the LORD has done this? In his hand is the life of every creature and the breath of all mankind." (Job 12:7-10)

Get out in nature. Be still and learn!

Wallace Murphy

One of the best teachers I've ever had was a college philosophy professor named Wallace Murphree. His class was an open forum of ideas, beliefs, and knowledge. He created a classroom environment in which students could believe anything, refute anything, and defend anything. Because we students were atheists, Christians, agnostics, and "undecided" the debates were very lively! That classroom was a free zone for thought, except for one thing. If you made a claim about truth, you had to name your source for that truth. You had to be accountable for believing it!

Little did I know that Dr. Murphy's philosophy class would be the genesis of my Faith in Jesus Christ. With all of the energy and passion of a 20-year-old, I began my life's search for the Source of all Truth! With the tools I learned in philosophy class, I dedicated myself to discovery. Wallace Murphy taught me to go after the Source! I challenge you to do the same thing! All your beliefs and values, all of your "truth", where did it come from? Your pastor? Your Mom? Your favorite author?

Truth is worth little, indeed is dangerous, unless the source can be identified. You can read the whole Bible but if your heart is not set on knowing the Source of its truths, all you have is dead religion! When we know the Source, we will begin to live from the Truth! Thank you, Wallace Murphy for holding me accountable for what I believe! "But when he, the Spirit of truth, comes, he will guide you into all the truth. He will not speak on his own; he will speak only what he hears, and he will tell you what is yet to come." (John 16:13)

No Bible Trivia

I've witnessed alarming statements from several acquaintances who identify themselves as Christians. They are denying that the 66 Books which make up the Christian Bible are authentic writings inspired by God Himself. They are claiming that some of those 66 books were included by white Europeans and are not from God. Some say there are entire missing books that should be part of the Bible but were deleted by church and political leaders.

But you know what, every person I've ever met who lived and breathed those 66 books confirmed their truth by the witness of their lives, lives lived with honor, conviction, and sacrifice. Through hundreds of years of history those beautiful saints paid the ultimate sacrifice by giving their lives because they would not renounce a single word of those 66 books, nor would they add a single word to them. By faith they believed the testimony of the martyrs who went before them who chose to die for me and you so we would believe those 66 books and give our own lives as ransom for the true words of God.

I've not seen one single person who denies the accuracy of the Bible sacrifice his life for anybody. This is only one of many reasons we can trust that the Bible we have, those 66 books, is the inspired and true, written word of God. It is in my heart to defend those words to the death. I believe that in my lifetime, I may have to.

"I warn everyone who hears the words of the prophecy of this book: if anyone adds to them, God will add to him the plagues described in this book, and if anyone takes away from the words of the book of this prophecy, God will take away his share in the tree of life and in the holy city, which are described in this book." (Revelation 22:18-19) Remember, we don't worship the Bible. We worship the One Whose voice the Bible captures!

Nothing Truer

Pick up your Bible today and ask God to speak to you through its words. To encourage you, here is why I believe the Bible is the true word of the true God—

1. If God is all-powerful and all-loving, would He not have both the desire and the ability to preserve His voice for the people he created? For reasons I don't fully understand, most of us don't get to experience God's manifest presence until after we die. His word is His loving, very real connection with us until then.

2. If the Bible is really God's word, then it's impact would be unmatched in all of history. It is true that no other writing has impacted the world for good like the Bible. It is by far history's number one best seller and most influential book.

3. If the Bible really is God's word, it would carry transformational power. The testimonies of millions across the centuries demonstrate the unmatched impact of the Scriptures on the human heart. Whole tribes and nations have been and continue to be changed for the cause of Christ because of its truths.

4. The world's most renowned archeologists agree that today's Bible matches the original manuscripts from the time that Jesus walked the earth.

5. The Bible is unique among all religious writings in these basic ways:

    a. God's word never demands, it invites. Every other religion has elements of control and manipulation.

    b. The Bible is the only religious book that proclaims there is nothing you can do to gain eternal life but surrender to God's heart through Christ. The Bible is the only religious book desecrated by satanists. Let's pray for them but remember, they know who the true enemy of evil is!

Today, open God's word and see into His great heart and mind!

"For the word of God is living and active and sharper than any two-edged sword, and piercing as far as the division of soul and spirit, of both joints and marrow, and able to judge the thoughts and intentions of the heart." (Hebrews 4:12)

Race War

Wealth will never willingly give up its place at the top. Poverty will never win the battle to get its equal share at the table. Mankind's contaminated DNA won't allow it. From the beginning of human history different races, ethnic groups, and religions have dominated, creating the disempowered. They generally didn't do it through legislation, ethical appeal, or rhetoric but through force like war and slavery. Are you so naïve to think that if black people came into power in our country that they would not become the oppressors? Whether white or black or red, oppressive rule is the natural response of un-regenerated peoples.

It all began in the Garden of Eden when God defined the new world order that Adam chose through disobedience.

The Creator declared of Adam, his banished original human, "He will rule...". And ever since, man has determined to do just that. Look at all of history! One people group came into power, owned the wealth, got too comfortable and got defeated by the next race, nation, or tribe. Even so-called Christians fell into this sad cycle of humanity by fighting conventional wars (the Crusades) for the purpose of the Cross.

No race of people will ever win lasting equality or prosperity through conventional warfare or human legislation. Our only hope is the government of God legislated by His surrendered sons and daughters. This can never be a government housed in buildings but one housed in the hearts of God's people.

The Bible says that the kingdom of God is like yeast that permeates everything. When you as an individual are true to your identity in Christ, you will automatically and dramatically spread hope, love, honor, conviction, wisdom, faithfulness, diligence, wholeheartedness, obedience, generosity, and the will to fight for these great values. The people surrendered to our great God are the ones who will rule the earth through obedience and devotion to the only true King.

"There will be no end to the increase of His government or of peace, On the throne of David and over his kingdom, to establish it and to uphold it with justice and righteousness from then on and forevermore. The zeal of the LORD of hosts will accomplish this." (Isaiah 9:7)

God and Galaxies

There are 100 billion stars in our galaxy! The average distance between them is 30 trillion miles. Can you even spell "trillion"? There are over 100 billion galaxies in the universe. (What's your street address again?) The DNA information in one amoeba, the smallest living thing, would fill 1000 complete sets of the Encyclopedia Britannica!

Whether you go big or go small, the complexity and precision of life on earth is mind boggling! That life is detectable scientific evidence for the creation of the universe by an extraordinary Designer. It takes far more faith to believe that the universe somehow just happened than it does to believe that a loving Master Creator was at work. It is good to remember that "chance" is only a word not a cause and that this magnificent God is attentive to your heart every single day! Listen to what He says about Himself!

I first met Christ on a clear, starry night deep in the country away from all artificial light. In those moments, if you can let your mind move your heart, you will see Him by His works! Because by faith we know that "He stretches out the north over the void and hangs the earth on nothing." (Job 26:7) "By faith we understand that the universe was created by the word of God, so that what is seen was not made out of things that are visible." (Hebrews 11:3) Phenomenal!

Good and Evil are People

I spent a few minutes yesterday with 2 Satan worshippers. They wore lots of satanic tattoos and symbols, including an upside down cross. These men did not slander Buddha, Confucius, or Mohammed. They did not dishonor atheists or agnostics. All their rhetoric and symbols were aimed only at one person—Jesus Christ.

Did you know that the worldwide satanic church routinely desecrates the cross of Christ and the Bible? Never the Quran or the Book of Mormon or Confucius. Satan's followers do not attack any other religion, religious figure, or religious writing. The stunning truth these 2 men unwittingly proclaimed is that Satan and his worshippers know very well who the Enemy of evil is.

Being a supernatural being, Satan knows truth on a level that we humans don't. He was there when man fell. He has personally met the Tree of Life from the garden of Eden. Your life is meant by God Himself to be incredible, impactful, and important. That's why the enemy of your soul is full of tactics and strategies bent on "stealing, killing, and destroying" everything good in your life. (John 10:10)

We need not fear Satan, but we cannot ignore him. His days are numbered but until then, the fight is on. Today maybe you could study these Scriptures that speak of Satan and what our response to him should look like. Most people who hate Jesus have no idea Who He really is and most Christians who never give Satan a thought have no idea who he is—two equally dangerous realities. (2 Cor.10:3-5; I Peter 5:8; Eph.6:12; James 4:7)

Where Does It Say That?

Here are 6 false beliefs that keep many Christians from doing extraordinary things:

1. "I got saved by saying the sinner's prayer"—the main point of salvation is a decision. The truth: The main point of salvation is the resurrection. Ours is the God of transformation—The point of the cross is change. (2 Cor. 5:17; 2 Cor. 3)

2. "I'm a sinner and God's in a bad mood about it". The truth: God enjoys me as His son/daughter. He

is the God Who is My Father—His heart is 100% for me. (1 Cor. 1:2; 2 Cor. 5:21; 1 Peter 2:9)

3. "I'm God's slave and He has my whole life already planned out." The truth: I'm God's friend and co-laborer. He is the God Who dreams—Dreaming with God is the highest calling of the human experience. (Psalm 37:4-5; John 15:15; Galatians 4:1-7)

4. "God overlooks my sin and looks the other way because He loves me." The truth: God paid a great price because of your sin, and we do too. He is the God of justice—The perfect holiness of God demands the perfect justice of God. (Isaiah 53; I Cor. 6:19-20)

5. "Sensual, sexual, and emotional pleasures are not holy" and my hunger for sex, food, victory, greatness, and beauty is selfish and wrong. The truth: God created me with deep longings that only He fully understands. He is the God of pleasure—With His guidance the most dangerous part of my life can become one of the most fulfilling. (Pro. 10:24; Rom. 2:13-16; Psalm 139:7-15)

6. "The supernatural power of God is limited in the Christian today" and though I see an occasional miracle I can't expect the supernatural daily. The truth: He is the God of miracles. The God of power—As a born-again believer I carry 100% of the power and authority of God. (John 14:12-15; I Cor.1:18; I Cor.2:1-5; I Cor.4:16-20

If you believe and live these bold truths, you will live a remarkable life of service to Christ!

Proof

Because an unexamined life is not worth living here are 7 irresistible reasons why I follow Jesus:

1. His life and words satisfy every longing of the human heart, longings for beauty, honorable purpose, intimacy without shame, to name a few. "For He has satisfied the thirsty soul, And the hungry soul He has filled with what is good." (Psalm 107:9)

2. Worldwide evidence of unmatched hate toward Jesus. From the satanic church to the jihadists to atheists. Darkness knows its True Enemy. John 15:18 "If the world hates you, you know that it hated Me before it hated you." (John 15:18)

3. The overwhelming fulfillment of biblical history and prophecy. It's there if you will take time to read it objectively. "This was to fulfill what was spoken through the prophet:

4. "I will open My mouth in parables; I will utter things hidden since the foundation of the world." (Matthew 13:35)

5. The universe. Christianity is not a mindless religion but is based on undeniable facts and overwhelming evidence of the creative design of the universe. "For his invisible attributes, namely, his eternal power and divine nature, have been clearly perceived, ever since the creation of the world, in the things that have been made. So they are without excuse." (Romans 1:2)

6. The witness of the martyrs. Many are willing for you to die for their faith. True followers of Jesus are willing to die for you for their faith. "If the world

hates you, know that it has hated me before it hated you." (John 15:18)

7. The heart of Jesus. Nobody honors human life and dignity like Jesus. Nobody. Completely selfless! "For Christ also suffered once for sins, the righteous for the unrighteous, that he might bring us to God, being put to death in the flesh but made alive in the spirit." (I Peter 3:18)

8. The conviction of the human heart. There is only one story in every human heart—God, good and evil, and hope through a Savior. If you look past all your pain and agendas, you know this is true. "For the wrath of God is revealed from heaven against all ungodliness and unrighteousness of men who suppress the truth in unrighteousness, because that which is known about God is evident within them; for God made it evident to them. For since the creation of the world His invisible attributes, His eternal power and divine nature, have been clearly seen, being understood through what has been made, so that they are without excuse. For even though they knew God, they did not honor Him as God or give thanks, but they became futile in their speculations, and their foolish heart was darkened." (Romans 1:18-21)

The Whole Story

John was born into an unhappy, unhealthy household in the South. A distant, angry dad made life at home very difficult. John was a shy, awkward boy partly because he was always the tallest kid in his class. It looked like he was destined for a mediocre, unhappy life.

But John kept growing and became a 6ft.11in. outstanding high school basketball player. After being recruited by several colleges he signed with Ole Miss. It was his time at college that changed everything. He met Jesus Christ.

He eventually married and had 3 boys who really grew tall! John became a key leader in sports ministry in Mississippi. God is using him and his wife in amazing ways in their family, our sports culture, and beyond! If you only knew one chapter of John's life, you wouldn't get the whole truth would you! What's true of John is true of you and me—we can't judge a life if we don't get the whole story!

John Engstrom's life illustrates a dangerous and unhealthy habit that we can easily fall into. It's not wise to take a verse or even a chapter of the Bible without connecting it to the whole story of God's word. So much harm has come to people, not to mention the dishonoring of the Lord, because someone took one Bible verse to prove a point or support a doctrine.

For instance—Matthew 6:33: "But seek first his kingdom and his righteousness, and all these things will be given to you as well." We prefer the 2nd half of vs. 33, getting "all these things", and maybe don't focus on what "seek first His kingdom and His righteousness" really means. This explanation can be found in detail in the sermon Jesus gave "on the mount." (Matthew 5 and 6)

May we all be students of God's heart and His word, seeking Him, His wisdom, and His ways. The Bible is like John, we can't get the full meaning if we haven't read the whole story! Is your Bible reading halfhearted and barely alive? Hit or miss skimming the surface? What needs to happen? Don't wait for an emergency in your life. Ask God to stir up the passion for Him that's already in your heart!

COMPROMISE

"If you love me, you will keep my commandments." (John 14:15)

Big Lake Biloxi, MS

Gatekeepers

The Great Wall of China is the only manmade structure that can be seen from outer space. 30 feet high and 15 feet thick, it stretches 13,171 miles along China's southern border! The Wall was built as protection against various nomadic groups, particularly the Mongols, a violent race of men who raided, raped, and tortured everybody in their path. This amazing structure was only penetrated once in its entire history. Someone bribed a gatekeeper and he let the enemy in! Tens of thousands died!

Adam and Eve were the original gatekeepers of the Kingdom of God, of all that is good and beautiful. Lucifer, the father of Mongols, bribed them and he has been raiding, raping, and torturing the tribes of the earth ever since! But in Christ, you have been made a gatekeeper! Your heart is the gate to the kingdom of God in you and no one gets in unless you let them! Here are some powerful verses about the gate of your heart:

- Whatever you value gains access to your heart. "For where your treasure is, there your heart will be also." (Mathew 6:21)

- Your trust in God is your greatest weapon against the enemy! "Trust in the LORD with all your heart and do not lean on your own understanding." (Proverb 3:5)

- Your heart is your responsibility. Your spouse, pastor, or best friend can't tend the gate of your heart. (Watch over your heart with all diligence, for from it flow the springs of life. (Proverb 4:23)

- The miracle of new birth in Christ is a transformed heart, a powerful weapon against the enemy. "And do not be conformed to this world, but be transformed by the renewing of your mind, so that you may prove what the will of God is, that which is good and acceptable and perfect." (Romans 12:2)

- You can expect God's leadership and provision when your heart is toward Him." And the peace of God, which surpasses all comprehension, will guard your hearts and your minds in Christ Jesus." (Philippians 4:7)

Lukewarm

Our head strength coach at Mississippi State University was Matt Balis. His workouts were the stuff of legend. Coach Balis promoted 4 rules for his weight room that defined his attitude toward winning:

1. No sitting.
2. No yawning.
3. Mississippi State gear only.
4. No cell phones.

As I got to know him, I discovered his values behind these rules:

1. No sitting—Leisurely, indifferent athletes never win championships.
2. No yawning—Your demeanor is contagious. Make sure it reflects dedication.
3. Mississippi State gear only—Be loyal to this family or go home.
4. No cell phones—Distractions are deadly to our cause.

Are apathy and indifference on the increase where you live and work and worship? With so many distractions and options, it's getting harder to be a believer whose life reflects wholehearted faith. The Bible has a name for indifference. It's called being "lukewarm" and the Lord addresses it clearly—"I wish you either hated me or loved me but because you are lukewarm toward me, I will not tolerate you." (Revelation 3:15-17. My paraphrase) Dang.

Lukewarm will never win people to the Lord or disciple nations. Do you need a Matt Balis in your life? Do you need to be a Matt Balis? "Whatever you do, do it with all your heart, for God not people". (Colossians 3:23)

"Thing" Love

I know a former college football player who fell in love with what the world was saying about him. From the time he was in middle school his family, classmates, and the press said he would be the next All-Everything. This young man started to believe it all and fell in love with this public persona. As a result, he wasted his amazing potential. A guy who could have been All-American wound up not even being a starter or finishing college. He went back home and became a drifter with no steady job and no steady direction. Though there are many contributing factors to his downfall, more than anything else, he got lost in his own bio. He got lost in idolatry.

When we think of an idol, we often think of the Golden Calf of the Bible displayed on a cart with wheels being rolled before the Israelites. But idols are far more every-day-normal than that. An idol is anything or anyone who becomes more important to you than God Himself. An idol can be a person, your church, or your body. It can be your reputation, money, or fame and celebrity. It can be the American dream and your retirement plan with that loaded 401k. It can be your hunting dog or your bass boat.

These things in and of themselves aren't bad. But we cannot value them above God and His will for us. I fight idolatry every day. No one is exempt. Here are some things we can check to be sure our love and devotion to God have priority in our lives:

- Do you ever question your loyalty to the Lord? If not, you are probably idolatrous.

- How much time and money do you give to your life's fun diversions vs. giving to help your church's missions?

- Who's getting the best part, the first part of your time, talent, and money?

Today let's do this together and be willing to make some changes—"Examine yourselves to see whether you are living in the faith. Test yourselves. Do you not realize that Jesus Christ is in you unless, indeed, you fail to meet the test?" (2 Cor. 13.5).

Nominal

In sports there's nothing worse than being on a team of athletes who lack commitment to the head coach. I was on a team once that started the season with a bunch of losses. People quit. Oh, they didn't leave the team, they just quit getting better. They quit on one another. They quit fighting for our values and goals. They quit on our coach. He was disrespected and our team rules were consistently broken. It was the most miserable season I've ever experienced. We became "nominal". I believe the largest and most important mission field in our country is that group of people described as nominal Christians. Here's the definition of "nominal":

1. Being such in name only; so-called.
2. Being trivial in comparison with the actual.
3. Far below real value or cost.

Jesus exposed "nominal" in His conversation with a prominent young businessman. (Matt.19:16ff) The guy was doing what was culturally expected but his heart remained unchanged. He liked to be known for being around the Lord, but he didn't have time in his schedule to discover the heart of the Lord. The worst thing about one being a nominal Christian is that we get them at far below their real value!

I know a man who is doing great things for God because one day he admitted that he was a nominal believer. He told me, "I realized that I sought the comfort of Christ more than the passion of Christ." To be completely honest, I have some nominal days of spiritual laziness too. But I have surrounded myself with hearty, hungry Christians who refuse to let me stay there.

What does passion for Christ look like for you? Are you experiencing transformation and helping others to be transformed? Ask the Lord about it, will you? We need the full gift of who you are in Christ!

Better Than Better

I watched an ugly high school football game this past season. Neither team looked disciplined or focused. In a postgame interview, one of the coaches surprised everybody with his summary of the game. He said it was the best game his team had played all year! He told reporters he had some young guys who had rarely ever won, that most of them came from tough backgrounds with lots of unhealthy distractions. He was thrilled with their performance because he knew the whole story and could see great potential that others couldn't.

That team reminds me of me as I was becoming a walk-on for God's team. In my first year as a Christian, I drank 3 or 4 beers most days. You might've been tempted to say, "He either has no character or is not even a Christian." Actually, I had a lot of character because I had completely stopped using all the illegal drugs that had been a part of my life for years. And I was most assuredly a Christian because I had genuinely given my life to Jesus. I no longer attended crazy parties and started learning how to be faithful to my wife.

Considering where I had been, I was living a very disciplined life. But my discipline was related to my history with God, not my relationship with you. I've learned that when I am patient and interested enough to get the whole story about people, I can begin to see great promise and potential in them instead of only their current messes. As we help people, let's start with the wisdom of God and not the three beers! "Do not judge according to appearance, but judge with righteous judgment." (John 7:24)

I was on a football team once that only won 2 games all season. Most of us players joined the team and wore the uniforms, but we never really got sold out to our head coach. We talked and looked like football players, but most of us never gave our hearts to become football players. People laughed at us, and I don't think I'm over it yet.

Wearing the Colors

Sadly, I did the same thing with God. I grew up in a God-fearing home, joined the church and wore the church clothes. I could talk and act like a Christian, but I never took responsibility to live like a Christian. I blamed everyone else for my problems but me. Many Americans are like I was, blaming everyone else for their problems while assuming no personal responsibility. There are many things that need correcting in our churches and country, but we won't get the win if you keep blaming others for your life. Don't be that irresponsible teammate who looks like this:

1. He will never give his full effort because he hasn't given his full heart.

2. He's an expert on everybody but himself.

3. Because he is divided in his own heart, he creates division.

4. He will let you down in crucial moments because he wants recognition.

5. Because he possesses a survivor mentality, fear and insecurity rule him.

6. He can't invest in others because he's never learned to effectively invest in himself.

7. He can't say "I was wrong" because he can't separate correction from condemnation.

DEDICATION

"Consider it all joy, my brethren, when you encounter various trials, knowing that the testing of your faith produces endurance. And let endurance have its perfect result, so that you may be perfect and complete, lacking in nothing." (James 1:2-4)

Cat Island, Gulf Islands National Seashore

Quiet Please

War takes a man places where no one can follow. I know a guy who fought for the US Army in Europe during WW II. If you ask him about it he gets this dreamy look and loses his voice. I've met a Black woman who picked cotton for a living until she was too broken to bend over. When I see her, she stares with dark, far away eyes. There's the young woman who has fought cancer for several years and, though surrounded by family and friends, always looks lonely.

As much as we would like to connect with these people, it is not always possible. They have fought on battle grounds we cannot begin to comprehend. The best thing we can do for them is realize we don't understand, we can't understand. That awareness changes my heart attitude from "How can I help you" to "How can I know you." That shift could be a healing balm for them.

"Great indeed, we confess, is the mystery of godliness: He was manifested in the flesh,
 vindicated by the Spirit, seen by angels, proclaimed among the nations, believed on in the world, taken up in glory." (I Timothy 3:16)

"And he answered them, "To you it has been given to know the secrets of the kingdom of heaven, but to them it has not been given. For to the one who has, more will be given, and he will have an abundance, but from the one who has not, even what he has will be taken away. This is why I speak to them in parables, because seeing they do not see, and hearing they do not hear, nor do they understand." (Matthew 13:11-13)

Where Does It Say That?

Beliefs that keep many Christians from doing extraordinary things:

1. "I got saved by saying the sinner's prayer"—the main point of salvation is a decision. The truth: The main point of salvation is the resurrection. Ours is the God of transformation—The point of the cross is change. (2 Cor. 5:17; 2 Cor. 3)

2. "I'm a sinner and God's in a bad mood about it". The truth: God enjoys me as His son/daughter. He is the God Who is My Father—His heart is 100% for me. (1 Cor. 1:2; 2 Cor. 5:21; 1 Peter 2:9)

3. "I'm God's slave and He has my whole life already planned out." The truth: I'm God's friend and co-laborer. He is the God Who dreams—Dreaming with God is the highest calling of the human experience. (Psalm 37:4-5; John 15:15; Galatians 4:1-7)

4. "God overlooks my sin and looks the other way because He loves me." The truth: God paid a great price because of your sin, and we do too. He is the God of justice—The perfect holiness of God demands the perfect justice of God. (Isaiah 53; I Cor. 6:19-20)

5. "Sensual, sexual, and emotional pleasures are not holy" and my hunger for sex, food, victory, greatness, and beauty is selfish and wrong. The truth: God created me with deep longings that only He fully understands. He is the God of pleasure— With His guidance the most dangerous part of my life can become one of the most fulfilling. (Pro. 10:24; Rom. 2:13-16; Psalm 139:7-15)

6. "The supernatural power of God is limited in the Christian today" and though I see an occasional miracle I can't expect the supernatural daily. The truth: He is the God of miracles. The God of power—As a born-again believer I carry 100% of the power and authority of God. (John 14:12-15; I Cor.1:18; I Cor.2:1-5; I Cor.4:16-20

If you believe and live these bold truths, you will live a remarkable life of service to Christ!

Water, Water Everywhere

Unless you played football when I did, you may not know what it means to be dying of thirst! Back in the day it was thought that going without water made you tougher. In the 95-degree heat and 99% humidity of summer preseason practice, we got only two small cups of water per 2-hour practice! I remember being so thirsty that I would try to scoop up some dew off the grass with my hands to wet my dry lips or suck precious drops from the cold wet towel the trainers gave us. Nasty! During those two-a-day summer football camps I stayed thirsty all the time. I even had dreams about water!

God's word reveals that thirst is an urgent spiritual reality. King David proclaimed, "As the deer pants for streams of water, so my soul pants for You, O God." (Psalm 42:1) A wild deer doesn't just want a bit of water. It longs for it and searches everywhere for it! Spiritual thirst is awareness of your own soul's deep need and longing for God. It's what happens when we realize that all our material possessions and human connections can never satisfy the deep desire that grows in our hearts.

Like my life in football, God uses your worst moments to show you the thirst that only He can satisfy. Don't go sucking on some wet towel the world offers! Receive the beautiful promise of Jesus—"Whoever drinks of the water that I will give him shall never thirst; but the water that I will give him will become in him a well of water springing up to eternal life." (John 4:14) As sons and daughters of God, we don't have to drink nasty water. We get to drink deeply from the thirst-quenching presence of the River of Life!

War Hero

It wasn't until the 1990s that Zofia and Andrzej Pilecki found out their father was a hero. As teens in postwar Poland, they had been told the opposite, that he was a traitor and an enemy of the state. They listened to news reports about his 1948 trial and execution on the school radio. But in truth, Witold Pilecki was a Polish resistance fighter who voluntarily got himself arrested by the Nazis and sent to the horrible Nazi prison called Auschwitz. There he started an historic resistance movement.

From behind those prison walls and barbed wire, Witold Pilecki sent secret messages to the Allies, becoming the first person to sound the alarm about the true nature of Nazi Germany's largest concentration camp. Despite extraordinary circumstances of starvation and violence at Auschwitz, Pilecki built a powerful and effective resistance movement that eventually led to freedom for all of Germany's prisoners of war! Though a prisoner himself, he guided the entire WW II allied resistance movement!

All Witold ever did was help save people and they killed him for it. Sound familiar? Jesus infiltrated enemy territory as a resistance fighter to free people from the prison of their own sin. All He ever did was heal and save people. Like Witold Pilecki He built a powerful resistance movement, the purpose of which was freedom for all who would join Him. What a beautiful gift it is to give something you can't keep anyway for something that you can keep forever! Jesus, the War Hero of all time!

Team Covenant

Coaches and athletes can't win if they aren't competing from the same core values. What's true in sport is true in life. "Team Covenant" defines a set of values that create the trust and loyalty that lead to success in sport and in life.

Team Covenant: The 10 Commitments of a Team Player

1. I will honor my teammates. (Honor recognizes and promotes the role and the value of everybody.) Philippians 2:3-4; Romans 12:10-12.

2. I will commit to thrive under authority. (I will choose to be coachable with a great attitude.) Philippians 2:7-9; Hebrews 13:17.

3. I will gratefully accept the position of role-player. (I am unafraid to take the lowest place or the highest place, whichever helps my team the most.) I Corinthians 12:12-26; Luke 16:10.

4. I will overcome offense quickly. (I will accept correction as necessary for personal growth. I will accept responsibility for my own hurt.) Hebrews 12:15; I Peter 3:9.

5. I will never stop growing. (I will learn to evaluate my own life for maturity and make necessary changes for personal growth.) Philippians 3:12-14; Isaiah 40:29-31.

6. I will be tough. (I refuse to allow negativity, complaining, or weakness to defeat us.) James 1:2-4; I Corinthians 16:13.

7. I will complete my team assignment. (Our team vision gives my pain purpose.) I John 3:16; Psalm 37:4.

8. I will pursue truth. (My value is found in my identity, not my performance.) Jeremiah 29:11-13; Hebrews 12:7.

9. I will anticipate great rewards. (I welcome the promises of a covenant life.) Hebrews 11:6; Philippians 3: 13-14; I Corinthians 9:24.

10. I will finish strong. (I will carry the burden of victory for our team, alone if necessary.) Luke 14:28-30; 2 Tim. 4:6-8.

DISCERNMENT

"For if you cry for discernment, lift your voice for understanding; If you seek her as silver and search for her as for hidden treasures; Then you will discern the fear of the LORD and discover the knowledge of God."
(Proverbs 2:3-5)

Barnett Reservoir, Jackson, MS

Blindsided

I once had some neighbors who enjoyed our beautiful coastal weather every afternoon by sitting out on their front lawn. Like a true Mississippian, every time I would pass them on the way home from work, I would wave to them. The guy always waved but the lady never did. I'm thinking she is a most unfriendly person. One day I stopped by to talk to them and discovered that she's legally blind! She could barely see my vehicle much less me!

Isn't it amazing how easily we can judge someone else based only on what we see with our eyes? God's beautiful word says that if you don't know Jesus Christ, you are legally blind. "In their case the god of this world has blinded the minds of the unbelievers, to keep them from seeing the light of the gospel of the glory of Christ, who is the image of God." (2 Cor. 4:4)

That unfriendly or mean person you meet today may not be able to see you at all! Stress, anxiety, fear, and offense make it very difficult to see the lives and the hearts of others. Don't take it personally. Because we know the One who sees, we can help them see! Jesus said, "For judgment I came into this world, that those who do not see may see, and those who see may become blind." (John 9:39)

Want clear vision? Before you look at someone else, stop and think about all that God has forgiven you for." "But solid food is for the mature, for those who have their powers of discernment trained by constant practice to distinguish good from evil. (Hebrews 5:14)

Skin Deep

Golda Meir was the world's fourth and Israel's only woman to hold the office of prime minister. Described as the "Iron Lady" of Israeli politics, she was a courageous and formidable leader of her people. Once when being interviewed about her extraordinary life she said, "Not being beautiful has been my true blessing. It forced me to develop my inner resources and be true to who I really am." Wow!

The mirror on your wall will be a curse or a blessing depending on the mirror in your heart. Never before has a civilization stared so long at its mirror while forgetting who we really are. No matter what your appearance, it is part of God's purpose! Beauty is in the eyes of the One Who beholds you! When He is enough you will be content about your own appearance.

But the Lord said to Samuel, "Do not look at his appearance or at the height of his stature, because I have rejected him; for God sees not as man sees, for man looks at the outward appearance, but the Lord looks at the heart." (1 Samuel 16:7) "Do not judge according to appearance, but judge with righteous judgment." (John 7:24) "And He will delight in the fear of the Lord, And He will not judge by what His eyes see, Nor make a decision by what His ears hear." (Isaiah 11:3)

Wrong guy

As a college student I won an award as the football player with the highest GPA. As a result, I was invited to an awards banquet where I was asked to speak. My speech was well received, and one individual even commented about how mature I was. She had known me for less than an hour! In fact, I was very immature in every aspect of my life. Here are some qualities that often get confused with maturity:

1. 1. Intelligence.
2. 2. Talent.
3. 3. Confidence.
4. 4. Ambition.
5. 5. Influence.

From my experience here are 5 things mature people do:

1. They make self-evaluation a personal value.

2. They pursue identity above image.

3. They make self-discipline a personal choice.

4. They seek truth above limited perspectives and personal agendas.

5. They inspire others by serving them.

Stop and reflect for a few minutes about your own maturity or lack of it. Better yet, ask your spouse or trusted friend what they think. That will take courage but also might lead to tremendous growth in your maturity.

"And Jesus increased in wisdom and in stature and in favor with God and man." (Luke 2:52)

What Was I Thinking?

I wasn't very well liked by my sports opponents in high school or college, and sometimes my own teammates. I ran my mouth a lot on the court, the field, and in the locker room. I have been in a significant number of "conflicts" that started with my own words. I wish I had cared more and talked less.

One place that is especially urgent regarding our words is marriage. This is particularly true when it comes to correcting your spouse. Before you correct your husband/wife consider these questions:

- In the greater scheme of things, are your correcting words necessary?

- Do you receive correction with the same conviction that you give correction?

- Do you consider the timing of your correction?

- Are you being helpful or critical? Your heart will tell you the difference.

- Your words may never change anyone, but your kindness and patience can change everything!

What God says about correcting—

- "Know this, my beloved brothers: let every person be quick to hear, slow to speak, slow to anger." (James 1:19)

- "Even a fool who keeps silent is considered wise; when he closes his lips, he is deemed intelligent." (Pro 17:28)

- "Whoever guards his mouth preserves his life; he who opens wide his lips comes to ruin." (Pro. 13:3)

I'm convinced that "fighting the good fight of faith" primarily means learning to bring our tongues under the leadership of the Holy Spirit. By God's grace and our faith, we can do that!

Openminded

The Bible doesn't tell us to have an open mind. It tells us to have the mind of Christ. Open-mindedness is often associated with the world's values and culture. In our culture it has come to mean acceptance of all beliefs, lifestyles, perspectives, and values. Jesus Christ never accepted anything contrary to God's word. But He did accept people. He was open-minded to the plan and purpose of God for all whom He met. He was open-minded to the Holy Spirit's leadership and knowledge.

I want to be open-minded like Christ, always thinking from His perspective. Don't let people narrow your definition of acceptance to having to agree with what others believe. That's not love. It's coercion. "Do not be conformed to this world, but be transformed by the renewal of your mind, that by testing you may discern what is the will of God..." (Romans 12:2) Love always speaks the mind of God at the right time with the right heart.

Here are some things I'm openminded to:

- Doing my best to understand your heart.
- Judging what you say without judging you.
- Valuing integrity and honesty more than our opinions.
- Showing kindness, which is the mark of confidence about Who and what we believe.

"For who has understood the mind of the Lord so as to instruct him?" But we have the mind of Christ." (I Corinthians 2:16)

"Do not be conformed to this world, but be transformed by the renewal of your mind, that by testing you may discern what is the will of God, what is good and acceptable and perfect." (Romans 12;2. See also Phil. 2:5 and I Cor. 2:14-16)

Learner

I know a high school baseball coach who saves a small portion of his monthly income in a special account and goes to every baseball clinic he can every year. Every day he reads something from other coaches about how to become more strategic, how to get the edge against rivals. He told me, "I can never get enough. I can never learn enough about how to coach baseball and how to understand kids."

He's been coaching for 23 years and not surprisingly is one of the winningest coaches in our state. Nevertheless, he is daily learning and growing and getting better! I want so much to be like him in my pursuit of God. Relentless. Hungry. Passionate.

I read the Bible every day not because I'm so spiritual but because I'm so needy. I pray throughout the day not because I'm a renowned saint but because I am so famously weak. Duty will never fuel my walk with the Lord, only revelation of His greatness and my desperation. "It is a trustworthy statement, deserving full acceptance, that Christ Jesus came into the world to save sinners, among whom I am foremost of all." (I Timothy 1:15)

God speaks to the learner: "I will instruct you and teach you in the way you should go; I will counsel you with my loving eye on you." (Psalm 32:8) "Whatever you have learned or received or heard from me, or seen in me—put it into practice. And the God of peace will be with you." (Phil. 4:9) "The fear of the Lord is the beginning of knowledge, but fools despise wisdom and instruction." (Proverb 1:7)

But I Thought...

I was a 21-year-old college student sitting at a banquet table with several other potential NFL draftees and one old man who was a stranger to me. Of course, we were talking about football. You would have thought we had been coaching for decades as we expounded on everything from offensive schemes to 3rd-and-long situations. As we were running our mouths, the old man just sat there, occasionally nodding and smiling.

Toward the end of the program, they introduced the keynote speaker, a man named Weeb Ewbank. Wilbur Charles "Weeb" Ewbank was an NFL coach who led the Baltimore Colts to NFL championships and the New York Jets to victory in the Super Bowl. To our surprise, Weeb Ewbank was the old man at our table. The whole time we bragged about everything we knew about football, one of the greatest of all time was sitting among us!

Can you recognize greatness when you see it? The disciples of Jesus lived with Him, travelled with, and learned from Him, but still possessed very little knowledge of Who He really was. (Luke 13) Sometimes our failure to recognize others says more about us than it does about them. Do we get so conditioned to the world's definitions and proclamations of greatness that we can no longer recognize the real thing?

Jesus defined greatness as little children with big faith (Matt. 9:14), broken-hearted women giving pennies that are still changing the world (Luke 21:1), and desperate parents who believed that love is greater than death (Mark 5:21ff). By the Holy Spirit, we learn to see Jesus, others, and ourselves from a Kingdom perspective, with spiritual hearts and eyes. Watch for Greatness! He's everywhere!

What's Your Source?

Who are you believing? Which news outlet? Which social media platform? Which political party or ethnic group? How do you determine fact from fiction and separate truth from opinion? Lately I have been given some dubious "statistics" and "facts" from some interesting sources, including our government.

For instance, if you are looking for statistics, causes, and solutions for poverty, you can find all kinds of radically differing information. So, who do you believe? I've observed that we generally believe what we have already determined to believe rather than the truth. It's called "confirmation bias"—the tendency to search for, interpret, favor, and recall information in a way that confirms or supports one's prior beliefs or values.

It is an important type of cognitive bias that has a significant effect on the proper functioning of society because it distorts evidence-based decision making. All of us are affected. Left to ourselves, we will never be able to identify, interpret, and apply the massive amount of information crowding our everyday world.

I believe the answer to this worldwide dilemma is of a spiritual nature found in relationship with God. The Bible claims, "But when He, the Spirit of truth, comes, He will guide you into all the truth..." (John 16:13) ALL truth. Not just Bible knowledge and theology, but ALL truth about ALL things. When the Spirit is our Source for truth and wisdom, we will stand no matter what comes our way!

Price Tags

I was recently told that if I didn't speak up on a certain political issue that I lacked courage. But when I did speak up and the person disagreed with my viewpoint, he told me I lacked courage! Wait! What? Don't ever let anybody define what courage looks like for you. In our culture, if it's not "courage" for their cause, your bravest stand will only ever be cowardly! Remember how the religious people mocked the Bravest Warrior of All Time because we wouldn't speak up for their cause?

"The high priest stood up and said to Him, "Do You not answer? What is it that these men are testifying against You?" 'But Jesus kept silent. And the high priest said to Him, "I adjure You by the living God, that You tell us whether You are the Christ, the Son of God.' Jesus said to him, "You have said it *yourself;* nevertheless I tell you, hereafter you will see THE SON OF MAN SITTING AT THE RIGHT HAND OF POWER, and COMING ON THE CLOUDS OF HEAVEN." (Matthew 26:62-64) As you remember, this was fuel for the murderous spirit already in the Pharisees.

And remember the story of the chicken and the pig? The chicken suggested they both be courageous by giving something great to the farmer. He said he would give an egg and that the pig should give a leg! What is a small offering for you may be a life and death offering for someone else! You're always going to run into that monstrous contradiction when you start trying to measure someone else's courage and faith with your own.

A man named Gideon was hiding in fear in the wilderness (like a chicken) when God called him a mighty warrior! He who knew Gideon intimately spoke greatness over his weakness and we all got to witness it! (See Judges 6-8) My courage is directly proportional to my obedience and only God knows what that looks like.

Mind Over Matter

One of the greatest influences on your life today will be how you process the people and experiences that you encounter. How you think, reason, and judge from your mind will lead you to either truth or confusion. If you are a follower of Christ, your mind belongs to the Lord like everything else about you. Therefore, it's urgent to think about what you're thinking about! Here are some truths to help you connect with the mind of Christ:

1. Salvation changes everything, especially the way you think. "From that time Jesus began to preach and say, "Repent (change your mind), for the kingdom of heaven is at hand." (Matt. 4:17). "And do not be conformed to this world, but be transformed by the renewing of your mind, so that you may prove what the will of God is, that which is good and acceptable and perfect." (Romans 12:2)

2. Fearful thinking can find no place in a mind preoccupied with God's love and grace. "God has not given us a spirit of fear, but of power, love, and sound mind." (2 Tim. 1: 7)

3. You are the one in charge of your mind. "We are destroying speculations and every lofty thing raised up against the knowledge of God, and we are taking every thought captive to the obedience of Christ." (2 Corinthians 10:5; also Col. 3:2)

4. The enemy's voice is full of lies about your true identity. You have to tell him to go in order to actively resist him. "For as he thinks within himself, so he is." (Proverbs 23:7)

5. Stop letting your mind take you down the backroads of your past. "That, in reference to your former manner of life, you lay aside the old self, which is being corrupted in accordance with the lusts of deceit, and that you be renewed in the spirit of your mind, and put on the new self, which in the likeness of God has been created in righteousness and holiness of the truth." (Eph. 4:22-24)

6. Right thinking starts in your heart from that place of intimacy with our good, good Father. "Trust in the LORD with all your heart and do not lean on your own understanding." (Proverb 3:5)

One Family, Many Races

Mankind was meant to be one family of many races, not one race of many families. As long as we prioritize race over family, we will remain broken. God isn't colorblind. Each of us was fearfully and wonderfully made by His loving hand. He made no mistakes when He gave us our skin color. Nevertheless, at the Garden of Eden, there was one family. Adam and Eve weren't a race, they were a son and daughter of their loving Father.

But then they went their own way. They wanted to self-determine who they were at the expense of connection with their good Father, at the expense of family. That arrogant self-determination continued in their descendants who tried to build a city and a tower called Babel, a monument to themselves. Instead of one family, mankind became many races separated and identified by rebellion more than color.

But God didn't quit on us. He brought man back to His family table through one covenant after another. His love didn't stop us. We continued to identify with race instead of grace. In Jesus Christ, the Father offered the final and most beautiful gift to us that we might be one Kingdom family forever.

We the people have made a mess of family because we have preferred race. We have allowed the Accuser of the

Brethren to separate us from the household of faith so he can destroy us outside the courtyard of our Father's house. We are living in fear and insecurity like orphans. We can't see the greatness in one another, only the differences.

How does our focus become one family of many races instead of my race of many families? Instead of responding with reasons we are divided, would you consider responding with ideas that will help us be united? Before you do, please read these verses that prioritize family over race:

1. "God shows no partiality, but in every nation anyone who fears him and does what is right is acceptable to him." (Acts 10:34-35)

2. "Have we not all one Father? Has not one God created us? Why then are we faithless to one another, profaning the covenant of our fathers?" (Malachi 2:10)

3. "And they sang a new song (to the Savior Jesus Christ) saying, 'Worthy are you to take the scroll and to open its seals, for you were slain, and by your blood you ransomed people for God from every tribe and language and people and nation, and you have made them a kingdom and priests to our God, and they shall reign on the earth.'" (Revelation 5:9-10)

Punching The Clock

LSU Football's offensive coordinator Steve Ensminger lost his daughter in a plane crash just hours before his team was set to take the field for the Peach Bowl in Atlanta, Georgia. Carley Ensminger McCord was among five people killed in Lafayette, LA Saturday morning as their private aircraft slammed into a parking lot and burst into flames in what's said to have been an emergency landing after takeoff.

The plane was heading to Atlanta for the Peach Bowl featuring LSU and Oklahoma. Coach Ensminger was in touch with his family up until game time but then he went out and coached one of the best games of his life as his offense scored 68 points to win the game. What does this say about this coach's priorities? Shouldn't he have abandoned the game and been present with his son in law in the worst time of his life? When I was a young Christian this priority list was driven home in my life by well-meaning people:

1. God first.
2. Family second.
3. Work third.

That looks good on paper but in real time it's not always wise or realistic. I don't believe you can prioritize love, devotion, and calling that easily. I'm pretty sure my family thinks my work often gets my best. I would agree. I just don't know how to draw a priority line through my relationships and my assignment. I also don't believe any of us can judge Coach Ensminger's priority decisions, or anyone else's. Here are some good priority questions to ask yourself:

1. Do I have an unhealthy need to be needed?
2. Do I determine my identity through my performance?
3. Does my family get less of me because I feel more confident at work?
4. Is my work a safehaven from personal or marital problems?
5. Do I lack a strong example of healthy work/family balance?

Be brave enough to have an open and honest discussion with your spouse about your priorities. Ask the Lord. Your time is so precious. You and your family are too!

God The Holy Spirit

The Holy Spirit will change your life as powerfully as Jesus changed your life! Sadly, most Christians have had limited teaching on the Person of the Holy Spirit and therefore limited experience with the Holy Spirit. Here are some Bible essential truths about Him for every Christian:

- The Holy Spirit dwells in the believer. He doesn't come and go. He is constant and poised to connect with you as you become aware and ready in His presence. (I Corinthians 3:16)

- The Holy Spirit will teach you all things. There is nothing hidden in the way of truth or direction that the Spirit cannot reveal to you personally. (John 14:26)

- You are able to access all of the love, power, and mind of God by the Holy Spirit who is in you. (2 Timothy 1:7)

- You can speak on God's behalf because you have the Holy Spirit without measure. (John 3:34)

- The Holy Spirit will not only teach you how to witness. He will teach you to be a witness! (Acts 1:8)

- God is working in you through His Spirit, giving you the desire to obey and the power to do what pleases Him. (Phil.2:13)

The Holy Spirit comes to live in us when we surrender our lives to Christ. But it's important that we welcome Him so that He can equip us and empower our lives for reaching the world. If you are truly hungry for Him, He will fill your heart and mind with love and wisdom! The second most important question anyone could ever ask you is "Did you receive the Holy Spirit when you believed?" (Acts 19:2)

Ambition or Anointing?

I'm one of the most competitive people you've ever known! When we are driving somewhere, Mary has to remind me, "Bill, these other drivers don't know you. They are just going about their own business. Nobody's trying to beat you to the next town." Like Simon the sorcerer in Acts 8, I sometimes get Ambition and Anointing mixed up. Check out these definitions:

Ambition—an earnest desire for some type of achievement or distinction (such as power, honor, fame, or wealth) and the willingness to strive for its attainment.

Anointing—set apart through the calling of God into His nature and heart for His purposes. (All followers of Jesus possess his anointing whether they demonstrate it or not. (See I John 2:27)

Neither is necessarily wrong, but it's important to know which one is motivating you at any given time. Here are some keys to discerning between the two:

- Ambition wants me to win. Anointing wants us to win.
- Ambition achieves. Anointing serves.
- Ambition drives. Anointing calls.
- Ambition is limited to human effort. Anointing is unlimited in God's grace.

The anointing of God is not just for people in the Bible like Moses, Paul, and Jesus. God anoints all of His sons and daughters! To live from His anointing, we are called to seek first the kingdom of God and his righteousness, so that "all these things" will be added to us. (Matthew 6:33) And let each of you look not only to his own interests, but also to the interests of others." (Phil. 2:4)

Entitlement*

When I was the chaplain for a college football team, I got to work with the incoming freshmen. I learned that there was only one thing that could lead to them not making it—a sense of entitlement. If they were bigger than the program, they either left or never reached their full potential. That consumer attitude got started through parents and family when those young men were just little kids. Sport can be an incredible teacher for life with the right leadership. Here are 5 things for parents to remember about sports and kids:

- Being rejected or overlooked is not a bad thing. It's one way God leads your kid to his/her true identity and purpose. Draw close to them in it but don't interrupt the process. Hard knocks fuel the fire of passion!

- Help your kids learn the balance between wholehearted effort and fun. The beauty of competition is what it demands from them through blood, sweat, and tears. When you remove pain, you cut the heart out of sports. Yet, if they aren't having fun in it, help them understand why.

- Preach and teach "teammates first". Train them up to be encouragers and supporters instead of consumers. A great question to ask after every practice/game, "How did you help a teammate?"

- Let the coach or a teammate be the bad guy. Be the safe place for your kid to cry, laugh, and process.

- If you care more about the sport than your kid does, then you are in danger of acting completely out of character. Sports is just one thing of many things your kid will experience in life. Let it simply be a growing and learning experience instead of preparation for "The Next Step" in their sports career.

*Entitlement definition—the unjustified assumption that one has a right to certain advantages and should be given preferential treatment.

ENCOURAGEMENT

"I sought the LORD, and He answered me, and delivered me from all my fears. They looked to Him and were radiant, and their faces will never be ashamed. O taste and see that the LORD is good. How blessed is the man who takes refuge in Him!" (Psalm 34:4-5, 8)

Back Bay Biloxi, MS

The Dawg Walk

The Mississippi State University football team experiences "the Dawg Walk" every home game. Two and a half hours before kick-off, the coaches and team arrive at the stadium. As they get off the buses thousands of fans greet them as they began the single-file, 100-yard walk through all those people to our locker room. Everybody is cheering and clapping. Fans close enough are high-fiving them, slapping their backs, or shaking their hands. They are calling players' names and yelling encouragement—"We love you, you can do it!" By the time they get into the locker room, about one-hundred people have physically touched and encouraged each one!

How powerful encouragement is and how little of it comes our way most days! It has been said that people need 10 encouraging words for every critical, correcting word. When I receive a word of encouragement from someone, it is life to my body, mind, and spirit! We need it and we need a lot of it to overcome the daily grind of life.

The willingness to encourage others is the responsibility of every Christian. "But encourage one another day after day, as long as it is still called 'Today', so that none of you will be hardened by the deceitfulness of sin." (Hebrews 3:13) Wow! The Lord ties a lack of encouragement to bad choices! No wonder. When we think nobody cares, we start not caring either and then anything is possible!

Love on somebody today by giving them timely encouragement—smile at someone, call out the gold in them, help someone in need, give resources, spend time, give a hug. One of the best ways to be encouraged is to encourage others!

Remarkable

His name was Pat Ludlam and he was a smalltown preacher. His congregation was about 40 people on a good Sunday. Nobody but his immediate family knew where he was or what he was doing. Nevertheless, he faithfully served those 40 in one of the most poverty-stricken counties in the South. Every week he preached and served and loved everybody he met. He never made the cover of a religious magazine, nor did he get written about in any newspaper. He just showed up. He showed up on Sundays at church, Mondays at your workplace, and weekends at your house.

He showed up at my house on a Sunday afternoon where he joined me for a short but epic conversation. "Bill, are those marijuana plants you have growing in those pots." (This was a day and time when what I was doing would get you 2-3 years in the state penitentiary.) In answer to my silence he said, "Bill, you know what? When you finally give your heart to God you will do remarkable things for Him and His purposes." I doubt if I'm "remarkable", but I don't doubt that that conversation changed the direction of my life forever.

I'm compelled to ask you, are you a Pat Ludlam or a Bill Buckley? Either way, it's time to make a difference. It's time to make a change. Here's to all you Pat Ludlams out there, local pastors and believers quietly loving people and calling out God's purpose in them. Theirs is the Kingdom of heaven! Oh and by the way, you're remarkable!

Kickers

For the many years that I was a football coach, I had a special place in my heart for the kickers. They are generally not noticed until they mess up, and then everybody notices. Reminds me of the parent experience. Mom and Dad give their blood, sweat, and tears every day so their kids can have successful lives, better than what they had. Nobody notices and few care, until they make a mistake! Then we crucify them by calling them bad parents.

I know that there are some parents who really are destructive and do more harm than good. But this is for the majority of you outstanding moms and dads out there who never get praised for the daily blood, sweat, and tears you give so that your children can experience their best life. Praying for you today that you will remember that the sum-total of your daily acts of giving and service will have an extraordinary impact on all of us! If you miss a field goal or shank a punt, I for one still believe in you! Here's some grace for you from God's word:

"The Lord is my strength and my shield; my heart trusts in him, and he helps me. My heart leaps for joy, and with my song I praise him." (Psalm 28"7)

"My dear brothers and sisters, take note of this: Everyone should be quick to listen, slow to speak and slow to become angry." (James 1:9)

"Rejoice always, pray continually, give thanks in all circumstances; for this is God's will for you in Christ Jesus." (1 Thessalonians 5:16-18)

"Do not be anxious about anything, but in every situation, by prayer and petition, with thanksgiving, present your requests to God. And the peace of God, which transcends all understanding, will guard your hearts and your minds in Christ Jesus." (Phil. 4:6-7)

"Be kind and compassionate to one another, forgiving each other, just as in Christ God forgave you." (Ephesians 4:32)

Burned Out Mom

My mother raised 4 boys on a working farm while keeping a 45-50 hours/week job her entire adult life. Her 4 sons raised and showed cattle, belonged to the HS band, and played sports every season of the year. She was always there. When she retired, Mom went home, sat down, and didn't get back up again. She didn't pursue any hobbies and quit volunteering at church and in the community. She didn't join the women's bridge club or the country club. She just came to a screeching halt.

I remember trying to motivate her to get involved with service clubs and the helps ministry at our church. She never did. I thought she was being self-centered. But now that I'm the same age she was when she "sat down", I'm seeing her from a new perspective. She wasn't self-centered. She was several notches past burned out! I now believe she wasn't healthy because she worked way too much for way too long.

If you know someone like my mom, maybe you can guide them to get help. If you are like my mom, maybe you could talk to someone like a good friend, your pastor, or a professional counselor. I don't believe that mom was happy the last 15 years of her life. She was too tired. "So then, there remains a Sabbath rest for the people of God, for whoever has entered God's rest has also rested from his works as God did from his. Let us therefore strive to enter that rest, so that no one may fall." (Hebrews 4:9-11)

Fan For Life

There was a season in my life after football that lasted about seven years. I had no plan, no purpose, and no place to go. During that time, I worked at several different "labor" jobs like hanging sheet rock, roofing houses, and working on a road building crew. I went from being a well-known football player to a so-called "common laborer". It was a painful experience when unkind people who knew me as a popular college athlete would openly laugh at the humbling turn of events in my life.

Tens of thousands of athletes will face "Life After Sport" this year. For some of them the transition will go smoothly, but many will not be able to gain a healthy momentum. This will be true because of many reasons other than irresponsibility. If you know one such young man, you will play a role in his future. You might stand by and do nothing, or you might earnestly pray for him. You could even build a relationship with him for guidance and needed resources. It will be work. But it may be one of the most rewarding things you ever done. Please, pray about it will you?

The number one thing these great young men need is strong, healthy relationships. What about motivating your men's group at church or surveying your community for organizations or ministries that are already working with young men? If you know of a program in your area, please share info with others. Let's get a plan now so when the season is over, we will be ready. We yelled for this kid's success on the football field, now it's time to get behind him in life after sport! If not you then who?

Enjoying God's Enjoyment

My grandkids enjoy me. Whenever I go see them, they run to me and hug me. If I sit down, they will sit close to me or even on top of me! They listen to every word I say and beg me to take them on some fun adventure. Our enjoyment of one another is one of my favorite experiences in life!

Jesus said children who have the capacity to enjoy Him and others are the ones who will inherit His kingdom. (Luke 18:16) Do you enjoy people, especially ones who are not enjoyable? One of the key reasons we need a transformed heart is so we can learn to enjoy people for who they really are, not just their crusty brokenness. We can maintain the conviction to see them get free of their sin and be mature enough to enjoy them in the meantime.

If I haven't learned to enjoy the Lord and experience His joy for me, I will have a very hard time enjoying people. In your life do you need to expose a false theology that teaches us only to be somber and sober in our relationship with the Lord? Does the love of God ever cause you to want to run to Him and jump into His arms like my grandkids do me?

Does not God's love for us presuppose His enjoyment and joy for us? His word says—"May the glory of the Lord endure forever, may the Lord rejoice in his works." (Psalm 104:31) In the beginning, God stepped back to look at His creation and proclaimed, "It is very good!" Nehemiah testified to the empowering quality of God's enjoyment— "The joy of the Lord is my strength!" (Nehemiah 8:10) Wouldn't you think it's impossible to take joy in someone without enjoying them? As we raise our kids, we take no joy in their bad decisions, but may we never lose the enjoyment of being with them. Just like our good Father.

Last Chance U

Bob Tyler was my head football coach at Mississippi State University. There were some MSU supporters and alums at the time who wanted to get rid of me because of my counter-culture ways. I was no poster boy. Not only did Coach Tyler refuse to run me off, but he designed an offense that highlighted my strengths as a receiver. He gave me opportunity in the face of opposition and my life was changed forever.

Is there a Bill Buckley in your life? The easiest thing to do is to get rid of him. Don't get distracted by the raw material of one of God's children! Design something around him and watch him rise-up to it! The Bible says, Barnabas "took hold" of this wild, half-crazy man named Saul and positioned him before the church leaders. (Acts 9:27ff) Saul became the great apostle
Paul and helped millions find eternal life in Christ!

Today, somebody in your life will need opportunity. You can help give it to them and it could change everything. Elevating others is costly. We're not talking about a handout but a hand up! You will need God's one-of-a-kind love, perseverance, and wisdom. "Now faith is the assurance of things hoped for, the conviction of things not seen. For by it the men of old gained approval." (Hebrews 11:1-2)

By the way, I recently saw Coach Bob Tyler. He is now 90 years old and I am 70! In less than a minute he once again elevated my game by telling me how great of an athlete he thought I was and how much I meant to our team and to him. In that 3-minute encounter, he called out the gold in

me in the way that only a coach can do it! Coach Tyler is
still directing my life toward success!

Belief Deposit

A young man walked into the Army Recruiting Center and
boldly signed up. As it turned out, he was only 16 years old.
One of 6 children of an abusive, alcoholic parent, he did the
only thing he knew to get away from a life of hell.

After discovering what the kid had done, his high school
football coach talked the Army out of having him arrested
for lying about his age. The coach then found him a home
with a local family where he lived until he graduated high
school. The kid earned a football scholarship, graduated
college, and began a coaching career that lasted over 35
years!

When I was 16, unlike the kid, I had good parents and a
good home life, but I too was living in a type of hell created
by my own fears and insecurities. I wasn't looking for the
Army Recruiting Center, but I was running hard from
being abused every day through the lies I had come to
believe about myself.

As an athlete, I was pretty much an "also-ran" until late in
my junior year when something happened that changed

the trajectory of my life. On the last day of spring football practice, one of my coaches walked with me from the practice field to our locker room. In those 5 minutes he told me I was going to be "a difference maker" on our team, to keep working, that he believed in me.

I went into summer workouts with a new fire in me and the following season was my best ever. Later, I would play college football and become a coach for many years. Oh, that coach who walked me off the field? His name is G.T. Thames, the 16-year-old kid who tried to join the army. What a powerful circle of influence! There are literally hundreds of us who owe him so much because of the influence he had on our futures.

I share this not for your entertainment but for your participation. Stay alert for even a five-minute window with a kid who really needs encouraging in the most important moment of his life!

"Like apples of gold in settings of silver is a word spoken in right circumstances." (Proverb 25:11)

Calling Out Gold

I had a coach who never gave any of us a personal compliment. No matter how we played, it was you shoulda' or you coulda'. His reasoning? "They will get 'the big head' and become lazy and self-centered." Maybe Christians are afraid to tell others about the great things in them because they are afraid of the same thing, that if we only encourage without evaluating, evangelizing, and correcting, people will take that as agreement with their current lifestyle.

Don't we have enough faith to give others our best encouragement and let the Holy Spirit do what only He can do? It's human nature to point out the negative but it's God's nature to point out awesomeness! "For since the creation of the world God's invisible qualities—his eternal power and divine nature—have been clearly seen, being understood FROM WHAT HAS BEEN MADE."—Romans 1:20 (my emphasis). That would be us!

How about we recognize "God's eternal power and divine nature" in everyone we meet! If people can get a revelation of Him in them or around them, it's usually enough for them to get a revelation of their sin—like when Peter saw Jesus fill his net with fish. "When Simon Peter saw this he fell at Jesus' knees and said, 'Go away from me, Lord; I am a sinful man!'" (Luke 5:8).

"Let no unwholesome word proceed from your mouth, but only such a word as is good for edification according to the need of the moment, so that it will give grace to those who hear." (Ephesians 4:29) You can change the whole direction of someone's life with only a few timely words!

Parent Generations

It was a beautiful spring morning in March when our first child was born. I was an agnostic, someone who believed you couldn't prove there is a God. But when I held little Carrie for the first time, I knew in my heart that God is real and He is good.

Everybody at the hospital was so helpful, friendly, and encouraging. It was almost like a welcoming party in our room! But as Mary and I left all that support and got in our car for the trip home, fear began to rise up in me like a bad fever. It was the dawning of a new reality. We were parents entirely responsible for another human being.

There were no parenting classes or great books on the subject. There was just that baby carrier with a live baby in it. Looking back through the lens of the years and 2 more babies, I feel a kind of gentle compassion for Mary and me and all the parents of the world. We made so many mistakes raising our children, especially me who had a load of my own brokenness to interfere. I had some learned parenting methods that were just not healthy.

By the grace of God and with the irreplaceable influence of Mary, our 3 children are remarkable and healthy adults who are now also parents. They are all doing a marvelous job at it! I'm so glad that they have access to child-rearing counseling, information, and wisdom Mary and I never had.

These memories have caused me to think of my own parents who had less parental training and help than we did. They did so much with so little. I wish I could tell them how proud I am of them, despite all their mistakes and failures.

As you read this and reflect on your own parents, I hope you will remember that the culture of parenting was not nearly as informative as it is now. I would bet the farm they did the best they could with what was available to them. Please forgive them for their shortcomings and failures. They love you more than you know. God bless the moms and dads!

FAITH VS. FEAR

"I sought the Lord and He answered me and delivered me from all my fears." (Psalm 34:4)

Gulf of Mexico

Bold As a Lion

Once when we were young boys, I spent the night with my good friend David. We decided to have some fun, so we snuck out of the house around midnight. We gathered up a bunch of dirt clods and threw them at a window in David's house then ran for cover.

After repeating this a few times, we suddenly saw a large shadow and then heard the blast of a shotgun! Terrified, we turned and ran for 3 blocks without stopping! After a bit we snuck back into the house and went to sleep. The next morning at breakfast, David's dad had a good laugh remembering our skinny butts running through the darkness. Of course, it was him and his shotgun that terrorized the terrorizers!

I don't know about you, but I'm alarmed at all the alarming news in our world today. It's like that shotgun blast in the dark every day! Do you find your heart running from every scary report about crazy dictators, coming socialism, rampant inflation, and the changing world order?

For the Christian, this is no time to be running! We have battles to win if we will remain courageous and faithful. God's word clearly challenges us regarding these times— "The wicked flee when no one is pursuing, but the righteous are as bold (confident) as a lion." (Proverb 28:1)

The enemy is a fake whose greatest weapon is fear, but you are the boldness of the Lion of Judah! My brothers and sisters, we are the righteousness of Christ, not because of anything we did, but because of Who He is! When everybody else is fleeing, we are called to stand our ground, to serve others, to give hope, to be lights, and push back darkness!

Keeping Your Eyes

Jack Tatum was an All-American defensive back for Ohio State. His nickname was "The Assassin" because of his extraordinary hits on receivers. Tatum was the guy who hit receiver Daryl Stingley so hard that it broke his back. He was arguably the hardest hitting defensive back of all time.

When I was a New York Jets rookie trying to make the team, Tatum was already an All-Pro player for the Oakland Raiders. We played a pre-season game at Oakland, and I got to meet him up close and personal. As a receiver, I would be lying if I said I wasn't concerned about Jack Tatum. I was averaging 3 catches per game, but against Oakland, I dropped 2. When Jack Tatum is head-up on you it changes your game.

There are two equal and dangerous perspectives we can have regarding an adversary. One is a minimize his abilities and the other is to have an unhealthy focus on him. If I haven't taken my opponent seriously and prepared well, I will surely get beat. On the other hand, if he is my focus instead of the goal line, I have no chance at all.

That scenario reminds me of "The Assassin" of our souls. I must believe in Satan's power to destroy my life, but I cannot get distracted by his strength. God's word gives us clear instructions about him: "Finally, be strong in the Lord and in His mighty power. Put on the full armor of God, so that you can take your stand against the devil's schemes." (Ephesians 6:10-11)

When our eyes are on the goal, the Person and purpose of Christ, we will stand against our enemy for "greater is He that is in you than he that is in the world." (1 John 4:4) What a great promise!

Moxie

Growing up I was way cockier than the average individual. I thought that was the way you were supposed to be, until the adults in my life told me different. I was taught during my formative years to believe that, before God, I'm just a worm and I should act like it. That's about when they lost me.

Around that time, I learned that in sports I needed to believe I'm better than you and can whip your butt. That idea created the heart conviction I needed to be a strong competitor. So, I graduated from high school and graduated from God.

In my life there has always been that tension between healthy pride and toxic pride. It begs the question—Isn't confidence a healthy form of pride? David of the Bible loved God and possessed great skill with a sling and stones because he practiced for years. This combination gave him the confidence he needed to defeat a giant.

For confidence to be healthy and productive it needs the filter of relationship. My submission to God and spiritually healthy people purges my confidence of arrogance. When your heart is connected to God's heart, your confidence helps us get the full gift of who you are. Like David. Here are some people who gave me confidence and what it did for my life:

- My Dad taught me how to use a gun and left me alone in the woods to see how many squirrels I could bring home. I began to believe I was his equal.

- As a 7th grader my parents completely turned me over to my coaches and never interfered with their leadership. I learned to fight my own battles.

- I had a high school teacher who showed me respect even though I showed her none. I realized that confident leaders create confident followers.

- A man bought an industrial cleaning franchise and gave me the keys to the company truck, knowing that I was only a year away from the drug life. I learned that confidence rehabilitates.

- When my wife was only a college girl she believed in me, creating the conviction I needed to resolve the conflicts in my life.

- The God of the universe put His confidence in me at the cross of His Son giving me courage to reach for all He called me to be.

Ask God to show you someone who needs confidence.

Somebody taught David about stones and slings!

Owning Your Miracle

I watched a security camera video of a kid wandering into the street. His mom brilliantly snatched him back on the sidewalk as a garbage truck barreled by! In his immaturity the little kid continued happily down the sidewalk, oblivious to the fact that his life had just been saved. That occurrence reminds me of the miracles of God. He is continuously, supernaturally at work around us, though we often don't see his hand in our circumstances.

We wonder why miracles don't happen like they did in Jesus' day. I mean, when is the last time you witnessed someone being prayed for and getting healed immediately? Do you know anyone who was raised from the dead or who was supernaturally transported from one place to another? Is God done performing miracles? I believe they happen around us every day though, like the little kid, we may not recognize them for what they are. Maybe it will help to identify them in specific categories like these:

1. Coincidental miracles. You really needed a bill paid and out of the blue someone gives you the right amount to cover it.

2. Everyday miracles. We are indeed fearfully and wonderfully made! Our bodies are stunningly designed to fight injury and disease.

3. Hidden miracles. Like the little boy and the garbage truck, God navigated you through mortal danger and you never even knew it. Think angels!

4. Ridiculously stunning miracles. Things like physical healings, people raised from the dead and set free from demons.

5. The salvation miracle. The impact of surrendering your life to Christ is the most amazing miracle of all! A new life, a new heart, a new future!

Do you need a miracle? Ask the Lord with an open, honest heart. He is a generous and compassionate Father! Believing with you for the miracle you need! In our materialistic culture sometimes the miracle is recognizing the miracle!

Go Get Your Stuff Back

Our Mississippi State football team lost to the Houston Cougars 74 to 0 at the Astrodome in Houston, TX. They took everything we had—our self-respect, our confidence, and our belief in one another. It was ugly as we became the victims of serious ridicule. Players got taunted and mocked by everybody from the media to fellow classmates, even our teachers and professors.

Two years later, on a beautiful fall day in Starkville, MS, we met a 13th ranked Houston Cougars team on our home turf. I remember running onto that field with the thought that I had rather die than lose this game. It felt like my whole life was on the line, and maybe it was! We had to get our stuff back—our pride, our belief in one another, and our honor. We won that game 27 to 13 and it became the most important win of my football career.

Have you ever gotten the dog beat out of you by your enemy? There was a time when the enemy of our souls stole everything of importance to me—my identity, the meaning of my life, my self-respect. Because of a lawless life, I was about to lose not only my wife but my life. Yet at the right time I had an encounter with Jesus Christ that changed everything. In Him, I came out a winner!

David of the Old Testament lost his family and all his possessions to a raiding tribe called the Amalekites. They stole his wife, his children, and every last thing he owned. But David, emboldened by his faith in God, went and got it all back! Everybody and everything! Read about it in the Bible—I Samuel 30. What about you? What have you lost to the enemy? Do you need to have a day of reckoning? Don't wait. Ask God for faith, conviction, and courage and go get your stuff back!

Dog Soldiers

In the 1800s, the Dog Soldiers of the Native American Cheyenne tribe emerged as dangerous fighting men who played a dominate role in resistance to the westward expansion of the United States. Dog Soldiers opposed the policies of peace chiefs and determined to fight to the death to keep their territory from the White invaders.

When fighting U.S. soldiers or other Indian tribes, Dog Soldiers would tie a rope around their wastes, then tie the rope to a strong stake. Finally, they would drive the stake deep into the ground. Dog Soldiers sent a clear message to the enemy—If you want our territory, it will be over our dead bodies! These fighting men represent one of the greatest examples in American history of unyielding courage and commitment.

What about you and me? Are we Dog Soldiers for God? What if we drove a stake into the ground of our marriage, our family, our church giving notice to the Enemy that we would give our lives to preserve and protect those precious to us. Jesus became the original Dog Soldier by driving a stake into the ground. It's called the Cross. He made a stand for you and me that cost Him everything! May we be faithful warriors like the Lord who refused to make peace with compromise and complacency. "But far be it from me to boast except in the cross of our Lord Jesus Christ, by which the world has been crucified to me, and I to the world." (Galatians 6:14)

Ready Or Not

Consider the End Times warnings we are hearing. Yes, a central message of the Lord is to live ready, that He is coming back, and all things will change. But how we roll that out can be the difference in the way people spend eternity. Christianity is the Good News, not the Bad News. If you must resort to fear only to reach others for Christ, then you will have to use fear to manage their walk with Him! That's what you call religion and legalism.

God uses warning, but all His warnings point toward His great love for all people! "It is the kindness of God that leads to repentance." (Romans 2:4) If you hear a warning that doesn't give people hope, then it is most probably rooted in fear not faith. Messages with instructions about gathering food, ammunition, and precious metals can be very misleading. If you gather all that stuff for your family and we really did have massive shortages, will you turn your back on all your neighbors who didn't collect that stuff? I don't think you would.

But if we spend our time seeking the Bread of Life, we know He will faithfully give us each day our daily bread. Darkness will increase but the Light will also! Truth and love are inseparable because they are a Person not religious concepts. "You must be born again" is Love's urgent invitation! "Arise, shine; for your light has come, and the glory of the LORD has risen upon you. For behold, darkness will cover the earth and deep darkness the peoples; But the LORD will rise upon you And His glory will appear upon you. Nations will come to your light, and kings to the brightness of your rising." (Isaiah 60:1-3) Wow! Now that's something to look forward to! Let's get ready!

Abraham, Martin, and John

Some of you will remember "Abraham, Martin and John", the old folk song recorded by **Dion**. It was a tribute to three assassinated Americans, all icons of social change—Abraham Lincoln, Martin Luther King Jr., and John F. Kennedy.

> "Anybody here, seen my old friend Abraham?
> Can you tell me where he's gone?
> He freed a lot of people, but it seems the good, they die young
> You know I just looked around and he's gone."

It's impossible for me to hear those songs and not feel my adolescent confusion about injustice. Three incredible leaders killed in their prime. How could we let that happen in a free and prosperous country? The lesson? No government, political party, or economy can prevent evil. But when God is sovereign in the hearts of a people, evil will not be tolerated. I'm not suggesting that we become a Christian nation. I'm suggesting that we Christians in this nation get completely sold out to the heart and the will of God. If even half the believers in America became radical believers, revival would come immediately! Let's pray these powerful Scriptures over our nation—

"For I will pour water on the thirsty land, and streams on the dry ground; I will pour my Spirit upon your offspring, and my blessing on your descendants." (Isaiah 44:3)

"All the ends of the earth shall remember and turn to the Lord, and all the families of the nations shall worship before you." (Psalm 22:27)

"And Elijah came near to all the people and said, "How long will you go limping between two different opinions? If the Lord is God, follow him; but if Baal, then follow him." And the people did not answer him a word." (I Kings 18:21)

Let Go the Banana!

In tropical nations the locals trap monkeys by carving a hole in a gourd just large enough for a monkey's hand. Then they tie the gourd to a tree limb. Finally, they put some fruit inside the gourd. A monkey will put his hand through the hole to get the food, but when it balls its fist to grab the fruit it becomes trapped because it can't bring itself to let go of the food! Who trapped the monkey? The monkey did!

This story illustrates a person putting his faith in God. Faith demands we let go of the banana (all our previous beliefs, relationships, and possessions) in order to find truth and freedom in the Lord. This releasing faith is essential in surrendering completely to Christ. Can we really trust the Bible as the authentic word of God? Jesus answered doubters of His day by giving this simple, yet profound answer, "My teaching is not Mine, but His who sent Me. If anyone is willing to do His will (let go of the banana), he will know of the teaching, whether it is of God or whether I speak from Myself." (John 7:16-17)

All those who desire to obey God will know by the very words of the Bible that they are indeed from God himself. I have recently witnessed so-called Christians saying that parts of the Bible came from man not God. There are dozens of reasons to believe in the authenticity of the Bible, but the starting place must always be complete, wholesale surrender of my life to His. The un-surrendered heart has no room for truth. "Every word of God proves true; he is a shield to those who take refuge in him. Do not add to his words, lest he rebuke you and you be found a liar." (Proverbs 30:5-6) Only wholehearted faith can comprehend absolute truth!

Harriet Tubman

Harriett Tubman is famous for establishing the Underground Railroad in the days when slavery was legal in our country. She determined to help Black slaves from the South escape to freedom in the North by identifying "safe houses". The slaves would travel at night and hide during the day in those predetermined locations. Harriett Tubman was the driving force behind thousands of slaves gaining their freedom in this way.

Sometimes a slave would lose his courage and decide to go back. Harriett Tubman would put a gun to his head and tell him, "You have two choices—keep moving north or die right here." She knew that the operation would be compromised if ever a slave went back to tell his owner about the safe houses.

In our faith we all need a Harriett Tubman. Being in the family of God demands conviction and the understanding that what millions of Christians throughout history have invested has become bigger than any one person. You can't turn back because we as a people/a family/a church can't. You can't give less than 100% effort because we as the family of God have passed all quitting places! Our road to freedom in Christ is a life-or-death situation. To turn back is to die to all God is and all He has for us.

If you see someone losing their conviction and trying to turn back from Christ, be their Harriett Tubman! Put a gun to the head of compromise! Abandonment of faith is no time for gentle answers. My wife came to me at the most critical moment of my life and said, "If you turn back now, you will die and take me and the kids with you!" I felt the cold steel of conviction against my temple! "Abandon lies, speak truth each one of you with his brother, for we are members of one another." (Eph. 4:25) You may lose a friend, but you may save a life, a family, a legacy!

Enemies

What if you gave a gift to your enemy today? He/she is a threat to you only if you allow them to be. Their control over your life is limited by God Himself. As a result, you get to bless them when they cause you pain and pray for them when they mistreat you. (Luke 6:28) Treat your enemies like you want to be treated. (Matt. 7:12) Love them by always returning healing for hurt, expecting nothing in return. (Luke 6:35) From my own experience, that is impossible without God.

Doing these things gives you a deeper revelation of God while purifying your own heart. (Luke 6:35; Matt. 5:8) God will restore and redeem all things. There is a season for everything. It is He who causes the sun to rise on the evil and the good and sends rain on the righteous and the unrighteousness. Know your enemy, not so you can plan an attack, but so you can win him! (Pro. 25:21-22)

Never take revenge. Be patient. Wait on God. (Proverbs 20:22) Don't fall into Satan's trap of taking vengeance or bearing grudges. Give over your offense to God so it won't destroy you. Remember, vengeance is His and He will repay at the right time with the right measure. (Romans 12:19) One of the greatest tests of your love for the Lord is being glad when your enemy succeeds and sorry when he fails. (Pro. 24:17) Believe it or not, you are a key piece in the puzzle of his life. Give love and forgiveness so you can be free no matter what he does.

Living The Impossible

In the middle of the night, Lester Marino Perez strapped himself to a wind surfing board on the north shore of the Caribbean Island of Cuba. As the prevailing winds carried him toward Florida, he was stung by jellyfish, attacked by sharks, and pounded by thunderstorms. If he had been caught by the Cuban authorities he would've been killed or maybe sent to prison for the rest of his life. For 48 hours he held on to that surfboard until the US Coast Guard spotted him 60 miles south of Miami.

He would later tell the free world—"No lie about what I was doing was possible." What would drive a man to do such an outrageous, fool-hearted thing? At the time, the Cuban people were suffering terribly under the communist regime led by Fidel Castro. They had no personal freedoms and Lester couldn't take the oppression anymore!

He is like all of us. We were born to be free. But freedom is risky business. Like Lester, we must make a decision to get off the bank of our safe, conventional lives and follow Jesus wherever He leads us. May it be said of me as His follower, "No lie about what he is doing is possible."

"And He said, "Come!" And Peter got out of the boat, and walked on the water and came toward Jesus." (Matthew 14:29)

GENEROSITY

"The generous man will be prosperous, and he who waters will himself be watered." (Proverb 11:25)

Catalpa Creek Mississippi

Generous Hearts

When our daughters were only toddlers, we had so little money that my wife Mary would regularly go to garage sales to buy our clothes. She never acted shamed, nor did she ever complain. She happily brought other peoples' clothes into our home for us to wear in the social-class conscience South! In truth, she was honoring not only God but me.

Though my life was a mess I had recently begun pursuing God and Mary was giving me the patience and the grace I needed to begin to take care of our family. She taught my girls that the difference in a good marriage and a bad marriage is not what happens to you but what happens in you. Thank you for believing in me Mary when most people didn't. It made all the difference!

From our experience, here are 3 truths that have kept us out of shame and in love:

1. We are not what we do and we are not what we have! We are a son and daughter of the King!

2. Our marriage is based on a covenant of promise and not a legal contract.

3. When we give freely without expecting return, all our needs always get met!

"Do everything without grumbling or arguing, so that you may become blameless and pure, children of God without fault in a warped and crooked generation. Then you will shine among them like stars in the sky as you hold firmly to the word of life." (Phil. 2:14-16)

"The generous man will be prosperous, and he who waters will himself be watered." (Proverb 11:25)

"For if the willingness is there, the gift is acceptable according to what one has, not according to what one does not have." (2 Cor. 8:10)

Extravagant

Years ago, I knew a man who was extraordinarily wealthy. He owned a Lear jet, vacation homes in beautiful locations, and several luxury cars. At the time, Mary and I lived in an apartment. We had nothing but a car with 250,000 miles on it. This wealthy man befriended us and gave us access to all he had. He flew us in his jet to stay in those beautiful homes. If he saw we had a need, he took care of it without us even asking him to. This man, who needed nothing, seemed to need us!

In the same way, God needs nothing, but by extraordinary humility has created in Himself a longing that only we can satisfy by loving and desiring Him. He who needs nothing has chosen to need us because He knows we need to be needed! Incredible!

"And may you have the power to understand, as all God's people should, how wide, how long, how high, and how deep His love is. May you experience the love of Christ, though it is too great to understand fully. Then you will be made complete with all the fullness of life and power that comes from God." (Ephesians 3:18-19) God is not needy. Ever! But He miraculously and lavishly positioned Himself through Christ to need your love!

The next time you are experiencing lack in anyway, remember that you are being "made complete with all the fullness and power of God". We must look at the cup not as half empty or half full but always overflowing with God's grace, wisdom, and love. When He is enough, we will always have enough!

Window of the Heart

I know a lady who gives $10 a month to a particular ministry. Not much you say? This lady who lives on nothing but social security is the most contagiously happy Christian I've ever met! Where does the joy in her life come from? She is a generous giver! The reason many people never experience her kind of joy in their relationship with God is because they give to Him only that which they can afford. But God never asks us to give what we are able. He asks us to give beyond what we are able. King David expressed this truth beautifully when he proclaimed, "I will not give offerings to the Lord that cost me nothing." (2 Samuel 24:24) When we give spontaneously and extravagantly, no matter how much it is, our faith gets engaged and God is moved. And when God moves anything can happen!

Why are we still talking about a widow lady who gave only a penny to God's work over two thousand years ago? The Lord was so moved by her extravagance that He chose her to become a part of His eternal story! Cheerful giving of our time, talent, and treasure is not only a responsibility, it's a key to life!

The sacrifice of Christ on the cross is His gift to us. Our sacrifice to Him is how we steward our time, talent, and treasure. What pleases God is a gift given with a cheerful heart—a great attitude full of compassion! There is no other action in the human experience that more accurately gauges our hearts than what we give and what we withhold.

Lord, drive out the fear and insecurity that keeps us from outrageous giving! "Whoever brings blessing will be enriched, and one who waters will himself be watered." (Proverb 11:25)

GRACE

"But to each one of us grace was given according to the measure of Christ's gift." (Ephesians 4:7)

Tibbee Creek Mississippi

No Payments Ever

Mississippi State University paid my whole college bill for 4 years. One of my close friends got no scholarship and finally paid off his college debt after 20 years! We both owed what we could not pay. My friend struggled for years coming up with what he owed every month. I signed a paper before I even entered college and it was a done deal. No payments ever.

Most of us work our whole lives trying to pay the debt for our mistakes, our failures, and our wrongs. We do good deeds, give to the poor at Christmas time, and try to get to church if we can. All the while Jesus has a full scholarship with your name on it. All He asks is for a full commitment, just like a coach asks for a player's commitment. Sign up from the heart and experience new life forever! Jesus paid your whole bill at the Cross! No payments ever! Thank you, Lord!

A Gift-giving God—

Matthew 7:11

If you then, being evil, know how to give good **gifts** to your children, how much more will your Father who is in heaven give what is good to those who ask Him!

Romans 6:23

For the wages of sin is death, but the free **gift** of God is eternal life in Christ Jesus our Lord.

1 Corinthians 14:1

Pursue love, yet desire earnestly spiritual *gifts*, but especially that you may prophesy.

Ephesians 2:8

For by grace you have been saved through faith; and that not of yourselves, *it is* the **gift** of God;

James 1:17

Every good thing given and every perfect **gift** is from above, coming down from the Father of lights, with whom there is no variation or shifting shadow.

When Shame Died

When I was a kid, I picked up a lot of shame. From neighborhood bullies, angry adults, and mean-ass coaches, I soon became what I was called—crowbait, piece of shit, and worse. It's stuff that happened to many of us, but for me there was never anyone who helped me learn how to navigate the feelings of worthlessness those remarks caused me. I never learned how to stop those verbal assaults from doing damage to my soul.

Nobody ever told me that God had a "No Shame" policy, that the reason Jesus Christ suffered and died for me was so that I would never again have to experience shame. Because I didn't know Him, I absorbed every shaming thing ever said to me and become a messed up, angry person. The biggest battle of my life has been overcoming my shame. But I'm slowly but surely getting the victory! What about you? Did you get shamed by parents or peers? Here are some powerful truths about shame from God's word:

1. God condemns shame. His heart is the complete opposite. Your name in heaven is powerful, beautiful, and holy. (Hebrews 12:2)

2. "Anyone who believes in (Christ) will never be put to shame." (Romans 10:11)

3. Ignorance of God is the place of shame. (I Cor. 15:34)

4. If you believe in, trust and obey God you will never be put to shame! (Romans 9:33)

5. The only thing good about shame, if we are honest about it, is that it drives us to our knees before the God who forgives and frees! (2 Thess. 3:14)

Ask God to help you understand if shame is playing a role in your life. You don't have to live that way anymore. Through Christ, shame died on the cross!

Boxing The Air

Mike Tyson was born on June 30, 1966 to a single mother. He is the former professional boxer nicknamed "Iron Mike" and considered to be one of the greatest heavyweight fighters of all time. Mike wasn't just a tough boxer, he was a violent man, having learned as a kid how to fight for his life on the angry streets of Brooklyn, NY. His father, Jamie Kirkpatrick, abandoned his family around the time Mike was born, leaving Tyson's mother to care for the children on her own.

Tyson himself has been married three times with 7 children who all became fatherless, just like Mike. All of Tyson's marriages were tumultuous, ending in divorce. In 1992, Tyson was convicted of rape and sentenced to six years in prison. Though it appears that Mike has become more stable and productive in his life, he has left a lot of hurt and pain in the lives of people outside the ring. I wonder how many of you out there are like Mike Tyson, wounded on the inside and fighting on the outside.

If I'm honest with you, sometimes I feel like a Mike Tyson, too broken even for God to fix, fighting for survival on the lonely streets of my own broken world. Like Mike, I learned to compete from a place of survival rather than mutual benefit. While other athletes were enjoying competition, I was trying to stay alive, or so it seemed to me. I don't want sympathy. I want freedom because I find myself too often with my back against the wall ready to take a swing at someone whom I think is trying to defeat me. Fighting for my own survival on my own is still very real in my life.

What about you? Why do you fight? If you're like me, we can pray for one another. One thing I don't need is another Bible verse about anger or love. I know all of them by heart. I need help remembering who I really am, a good son of a good Father. As sons and daughters of the living God we were certainly created to fight, but it's called "the good fight of faith" and our weapons are surrendered hearts, not angry words.

Let's pray for one another, OK? Let's take our hands off that switch that ignites anger into words and actions. With lots of anger in my past and it's attending shame, I've had to learn how it looks and feels to be kind to myself, just like our good Father is kind to us. That's a game-changer right there! Let's stop boxing the air and lay some punches to the chin of the real enemy!

Disciplining/punishing a person for anger by withholding something will never change them. Repentance for hurting others is essential but we will never win that battle if we don't first defeat the shame and self-loathing we already carried. (I Cor. 9:26)

Flea-bitten Faith

I watched a lady rescue a dog that had been chained to a stake in the ground for its whole life. The dog was close to death from starvation and had no light in her eyes. It was giving up the fight. But the lady was committed. After a trip to the vet, she bathed what was left of this mangy dog, gave her a warm place to sleep, and fed her healthy food full of vitamins.

In her new home she experienced freedom for the first time. She had been chained to that stake in the ground for so long that she literally could only walk in circles! This kind lady named the dog Frida, which is German for "freedom", and loved on her with tenderness and affection.

The transformation was amazing! Frida quickly gained weight, grew a beautiful coat of hair, and learned to walk in a straight line. The light came back into her eyes! Not surprisingly, the dog worshipped its new master and wanted to be with her every minute.

How could anything so ugly become so beautiful? The touch of her master's hand! Frida's life parallels my own. I had to get rescued because I was a mangy stray too, chained by Satan and spiritually malnourished with no light in my eyes. My life was nothing but circles.

Now, when I meet someone who does not know Jesus, I see in my mind's eye the image of that starving, chained dog. And I remember what The Lord did for me—"being rich in mercy, because of the great love with which he loved us, even when we were dead in our trespasses, made us alive together with Christ—by grace you have been saved— and raised us up with him and seated us with him in the heavenly places in Christ Jesus" (Eph 2:4-6). Free to walk straight! Lord, give us eyes to see the true spiritual health of people. Help us to find the courage and commitment to go rescue them!

Failure—God's Birthing Suite

You and I have an important part to play in the redemption of fellow Christians who have experienced moral failure. It's one thing to fail as a non-believer but a very different thing to fail as a Christian. We often have more grace for the non-believer than our brother or sister in Christ who falls. Maybe it's because salvation/redemption stories are beautiful in their freshness while shame tends to pursue the brother who cheated on his wife. But redemption is redemption, no matter the circumstances.

King David was guilty of breaking half of God's commandments. He coveted Uriah's wife (2 Sam. 11:2-3), committed adultery with her (2 Sam. 11:4) effectively stealing her from Uriah (2 Sam. 12:9), lying to him (2 Sam. 11:12–13) , and eventually having him murdered (2 Sam. 12:9). But David repented and experienced God's full restoration. The principle? With God, failure doesn't get the last word!

Remember the disciple John Mark who quit when the going got rough? (Acts 12, 13) God used him to write one of the Gospel books! The principle? We all develop gradually. Failure isn't always a sign that we can't cut it. Sometimes we're trying to operate at a level that we're not mature enough to handle. We can always outgrow those kinds of failings, provided we don't give up and others don't give up on us. And how about Peter who publicly denied that he was a follower of Christ. He showed us that failure doesn't disqualify you, even if you've been following Jesus for some time.

There is someone in your life who God is seeking to restore. You can be a part of their story by earnestly praying for them. Privately find out where they are in the redemption process. Ask God for the wisdom to lovingly intervene. There are a bunch of soldiers of Christ out there with self-inflicted wounds. We have a responsibility to go to them and bring them back home.

Response Time

What coaches tell athletes is true for you and me—If you get in the game long enough, you're going to make a mistake. A fumble, a dropped pass, an interception, a missed tackle or missed block, maybe a missed field goal. Nobody plays the perfect game. Most likely the mistake is not what will get us beat. It's your response to the mistake that gets us beat.

Responses like frustration, embarrassment, blaming a teammate or coach—reactions that shut you down and take you out of the game. If we are going to win, we got to avoid these momentum-killing responses. When you make a mistake—

1. Remember who you are. Stay true to your identity and don't let a mistake define you.

2. Remember who we are. Don't let mistakes destroy unity with your coaches and teammates.

3. If a teammate makes a mistake, go get him back in the game.

4. Prepare your mind for action. Get your head right and stay focused on the big picture.

5. Set your heart. Show up prayed up. Ask the Lord for strength and courage.

There's only one who never made a mistake, the One who died for your mistakes—Jesus Christ, the original Champion! "Brothers, there's one thing that will give us victory, forgetting what lies behind and straining forward to what lies ahead, we press on toward the goal to win the

prize laid out before us both here on earth and in heaven."
(Philippians 4:13-14)

Out Of My League

One of my major shortcomings as a parent is my inability to recognize, evaluate, and help my kids with their emotional needs. It's not because I didn't care. It's because my family of origin did not have any template for even what emotional needs look like, much less how to help someone navigate them in a healthy way.

Sometimes my parents would angrily say something like, "If you think you're in a bad mood now, just keep at it. I'll put you in a really bad mood!" Or "Stop crying or I'll give you something to cry about. Go outside and find something to do!"

It sounds uncaring but they were just giving us what they had learned. Their anger was sometimes more from frustration than it was about us kids. They didn't have any training or experience with emotional health either. There was no mentoring in these matters back in the day, only an unspoken will and determination to survive.

I am trying to grow in this area because I love my kids and because I am a learner. But even now it's not easy to gain that kind of information in a helpful and clear way, not to mention possessing the knowledge to help heal old hurts caused by my inadequacies. So, please reconsider the way you relate to your parents about these challenging issues. I guarantee you they only want what's best for you. Sometimes they just don't know what that looks like.

Parents let's don't stop learning. Don't use your ignorance as an excuse. I know I've got to stop being defensive when my kids point out my dysfunctional ways of handling strong emotions. We need so much understanding on both sides. Help us Lord!

Idiots

What if your attitude with obnoxious people went from "Who do you think you are?" to "Let me tell you who you are." Jesus had a chance to call many people an idiot, but he usually saw the best in them and then told them about it. That takes a lot of confidence and courage. A good attitude is like a healing balm, especially for the one who carries it.

I met a young man on the street this week who acted like he wanted to fight. Because I was prepared, I was able to tell him a couple of things about himself that only God would know. We went from almost fighting to hugging. He quickly became like the lost puppy that he was and didn't want me to leave him. God showed me that his arrogance was really the pain he felt from a long history of not being loved.

Remember when Simon cut a guy's ear off trying to defend the Creator of the Universe? I think that qualifies as an idiot! Then, not long after that, when things started to heat up around the Christ's crucifixion, Simon denied that he knew the Lord. He hated himself for what he had done but the next time we hear Jesus talking about him, our Redeemer not only does not shame him, but calls out the greatness in him by giving him a new name, and eventually a new heart! It was from failure that Peter was born!

Next time you want to call someone an idiot, take a moment and remember Simon Peter. Remember Jesus. Be of a different Spirit. Demand your anger and offense serve the Lord. I have failed at this too many times, but I will never give up the fight to let Christ have His way in my attitude toward others.

Precious Mettle

Mary and I hit the streets occasionally searching out homeless people. One night we agreed that we would give 40 bucks to each of them until our money ran out. These people are conditioned to getting maybe a couple bucks from others. The first guy hugged me and told us how he would be able to get a room and a shower that night. All the others wept openly!

Kindness inspired from God's great heart can reach the coldest heart. Nice, helpful, friendly, pleasant—great qualities all but none of them define this kindness of God. Here's how the Bible describes it:

- Kindness is extravagant mercy. It's one thing to show an act of mercy but another entirely to love mercy. Kindness is the difference! (Micah 6:8)

- Kindness is like clothing. We have to remember to put it on every morning. (Colossians 3:12)

- Kindness and truth are inseparable. The greatest hindrance to evangelism is when we share one but never share the other. (Pro. 3:3)

- Kindness will lead to a changed heart faster than anything. (Romans 2:4)

- Discipline and correction are kindness if inspired by the Holy Spirit. (Psalm 141:5)

- Be especially kind to the unkind. It's the one thing they need more than anything else. (Luke 6:35)

- Genuine kindness will break a heart in the right places. (Titus 3:4)

It's so easy to put a bumper sticker on your life—"Be Kind." But honestly? If I fail to submit to God's power and leadership, I have zero chance of being consistently kind to all people all the time. Help me, Lord!

Nowhere To Go

I'm sure you've seen those homeless people out on the streets talking to nobody but themselves. I have spent much time with them and with people who knew them before they forgot who they were. This one lady, Joan, was a very beautiful woman, though the streets had robbed her brilliance. I learned that she was a successful marketing VP living beyond her willpower. Someone introduced her to fentanyl and in a matter of days she was completely overpowered by addiction. In only a few months she went from making 7 figures to shuffling down city streets! One decision. Zero warning. No safety net. Money, pride, and DNA.

Today she had this stunned look in her eyes as if she had suddenly arrived in some strange land and couldn't find her way home. I am deeply saddened by Joan's life, not only because of Christ in me, but because she is me. I also made that one decision that ruled all others. The one that would take me over the edge of what I used to be and what I could have been. The only difference in her and me was a few people who chose to enter my life in the timeliest of ways.

Be alert! There is only a thin line of sanity between you and me and Joan. We are no different, just one decision over. Jesus is the great hope for a homeless planet, and you can help. We don't have to be empty handed when we meet people on the street. From my own experience, here are some things you can do when you see the homeless or the poor:

1. Look them in the eye and ask them their first name. Give them a big smile, even if you don't give them anything else. To avoid them only makes you feel guilty.

2. Pray inwardly for them and ask God to break your heart over them.

3. If you're courageous enough, you might ask them how you can pray for them. Ask them if you can pray with them on the spot.

4. Offer to buy them a meal. It's probably best to go buy it yourself rather than give them the money, though I have occasionally given cash.

5. Ask them if you can hug them. Tell them you will be thinking about them and praying for them.

6. Be a part of your church's homeless ministry. (If your church doesn't have a homeless ministry or ministry to the poor maybe you can start one.)

7. Serve with homeless ministries already working in your city.

Listen to God's heart for these precious people—

"He raises the poor from the dust and lifts the needy from the ash heap; he seats them with princes and has them inherit a throne of honor. 'For the foundations of the earth are the Lord's; on them he has set the world.'" (I Samuel 2:8)

Be His hands and feet to the homeless! Don't pass them by.

Sinners in the Hands of a Loving God

Check out these scary Scripture verses about God's wrath:

"For the wrath of God is revealed from heaven against all ungodliness and unrighteousness of men, who by their unrighteousness suppress the truth." (Romans 1:18)

"Whoever believes in the Son has eternal life; whoever does not obey the Son shall not see life, but the wrath of God remains on him." (John 3:36)

How you define the wrath of God determines who you believe God to be. The Bible defines God as love not wrath, so how do we process verses like the ones above? Here are some thoughts about this challenging subject—

1. The object of God's wrath has always been sin, not people. The power of sin was destroyed by the sacrifice of Jesus at the cross. All who carry Jesus are never under God's wrath. All who don't carry Jesus are always under God's wrath, not because He hates you but because He loves you. "He who believes in the Son has eternal life; but he who does

not obey the Son will not see life, but the wrath of God abides on him." (John 3:36)

2. God's wrath and His anger are not the same. His wrath is reserved for the conviction of all who don't know Jesus, His anger for the correction of His sons and daughters. "For God has not destined us for wrath, but for obtaining salvation through our Lord Jesus Christ." (I Thess.5:9) (See also John 3:36 above).

3. God's wrath does not contradict His love. It expresses His love. He has a personal agenda against anything that hinders love, anything that hurts people. Sin causes emotional, physical, and relational pain and separation. He is a good Father, restoring health to a world full of the pain of sin! (2 Chron. 7:14; John 3:16-17)

4. God has already judged sin through the cross of Christ. Many say He's judging our nation because of sin. Well, that's not biblically accurate. He judged sin once for all through Christ. The coming judgement is not about sin but about whether or not you know Jesus Christ. "The last days" began 2000 years ago at Pentecost and are marked by the supernatural love and power of God—a loving Father restoring people to Himself, not holding their sins against them. (Acts 2:17-21; 2 Cor. 5:17-19) On "the last day" (the return of Jesus—Malachi 4;5), Jesus will judge everyone as to whether or not they carry Him in their hearts. At that moment, all will know whether or not they chose eternity with the Father or eternity without him.

Zero Failure Rate

If we were completely honest, most of us would have to say that we give people just one chance. If they hurt us, treat us unjustly or unkindly, we shut them out of our lives. We might be polite to them, but we no longer give them access to our hearts. While I believe that sometimes it's necessary to set a boundary with someone who has intentionally hurt us, we don't have to give up on them.

As a man like us, Jesus had limitations. He needed nourishment—both spiritual and physical. He rested and he was aware that some people could not be trusted. (John 2:23-25) Nevertheless He never abandoned others. Here are a few ways the Lord set healthy, hopeful boundaries:

1. He set prayer as a priority. (Luke 5:16)

2. Jesus taught to be confident in your "yes's" and "no's." This confidence is available to us who are actively pursuing His heart. (Matthew 5)

3. Jesus expected others to be open and honest with Him. Remember his question for the blind guy? "What do you want me to do for you?'"—Matthew 20:30, 32

The Holy Spirit doesn't teach us to always be nice, He teaches us how to always love wisely. If you mistreated me, I may not give you the same access to my life as you once had, but I will never give up on our relationship. Because I believe that love never fails. Here are three things you must give up to not give up on those who have hurt you:

1. Offense. Offense is a form of punishment for both you and the one you are offended at.

2. Control. I can be strong in the Lord without being manipulative.

3. Pride. Humility may be the most important trait for all who claim to love others.

Butt Ugly

It's a problem of mass proportions in our time—people holding other people accountable for their own offense. If you are offended at someone, you are solely responsible to confront and release that offense, no matter what the one who offended you chooses to do. If you can't do that, you will always be a slave to that individual or group of people who offended you.

God allows you to hold the key to your own freedom. Justice will never be served through your offense only through your forgiveness. If your heart carries bitterness and resentment against any group, race, or person you have become your own worst enemy, not to mention all whom you rail against.

People are not your problem. Anytime you relate to others outside of God's guidance as defined by love, joy, peace, patience, kindness, goodness, gentleness, faithfulness, and self-control, then you become the problem. If you demand justice, your offense will never move the needle. Ask God to search your heart for offense. Ask someone not on your "team" if they think that you are an offended person. Here is what God's word says about it—

1. "One who is offended is more unyielding than a strong city, and quarreling is like the bars of a castle." (Proverb 18:19)

2. "Bless those who curse you, pray for those who abuse you. To one who strikes you on the cheek, offer the other also, and from one who takes away your cloak do not withhold your tunic either." (Luke 6:28)

3. "When he was hated, he did not hate in return; when he suffered, he did not threaten, but continued entrusting himself to Him who judges justly." (I Peter 2:23)

4. "Cast your burden on the Lord, and he will sustain you; he will never permit the righteous to be moved." (Psalm 55:22)

5. "Be angry and do not sin; do not let the sun go down on your anger, and so give no opportunity to the devil." (Eph. 4:26-27)

Lots of practical advice in these powerful verses. Take some of these Spirit-inspired steps and get free of offense! You're a whole lot better looking when you aren't bitter!

GUIDANCE

"But when He, the Spirit of truth, comes, He will guide you into all the truth. He will not speak on his own; He will speak only what He hears, and He will tell you what is yet to come." (John 16:13)

Tombigbee River Columbus, Mississippi

Am I Lost?

I was fulfilling a wish of my 7-year-old grandson Judah. He
wanted us to kayak "further than we've ever been! All the
way to Popps Ferry Bridge!" So, we set out in my tandem
kayak with him in front and me behind. It was hard work
because the weather was cloudy and rainy. About halfway
out above the wind and rain I heard Judah ask, "Papa, am I
lost?" I laughed to myself at his childlike question until I
remembered how often I've asked my Father in heaven the
same thing! I told Judah, "Of course you're not lost
because I'm not! I know exactly where we are and exactly
where we are going. Be at peace and enjoy the ride!" After
assuring him we were on the right course, we paddled all
the way to Popp's Ferry Bridge and back!

When we got back home, Judah walked in the door with
his chest stuck out bragging to his mama about how far we
went! Have you ever asked God that question! "Lord, am I
lost?" or "Lord, I'm surely lost!" His answer is the same one
I gave Judah, "No, my son/daughter, you're not lost
because I'm not lost!" What God has called you to, He will
see you through. Though we may not understand our
current position, our God is "the beginning and the end!"

Don't forget that He cares about your hopes and dreams,
and once you get off the bank of indecision and go for it,
He will not forsake you! "Behold, I am with you and will

keep you wherever you go and will bring you back to this land. For I will not leave you until I have done what I have promised you." (Genesis 28:15)

Christian Luck

I saw a vanity license plate yesterday that read "LUCKY 13". And then below it on the tag holder was written "In God we trust." That car tag represents one of the biggest problems we have in understanding the heart and mind of God. Was it just luck that I was born into a white middle class culture and not an impoverished family in India's caste system? When my friend gets cancer and I do not, is that just the roll of the dice? How you view these things determines your response to adversity and reflects who you believe God to be.

We cannot always determine whether God's active or passive will is involved in the events of our lives, but we do know that all things that take place are under His purposeful will. As a result, though some circumstance may not have been initiated by Him, He will always use it for our ultimate good. Remember, He is love.

When a person rolls the dice to play a board game, God may sometimes cause the dice to land a certain way, but in such inconsequential matters, He may allow the dice to land as His laws of nature would determine without any active involvement. But even when He is not actively involved, how the dice land is still under His eyes and His plan.

So it is for any event of life. No matter how small (Matthew 10:29-31) or how large (Daniel 4:35; Proverbs 21:1), God is sovereign over all (Ephesians 1:11; Psalm 115:3; Isaiah 46:9-10), and thus one is hard-pressed to claim something is a matter of chance. From an earthly perspective, things may seem to happen at random, but throughout the whole of Scripture, it is clear that God is in control of all of His creation and is somehow able to take the random acts of natural law, the free will of both good and evil men, and the wicked intent of demons and combine them all to accomplish His good and perfect will! (Genesis 50:20; Job chapters 1 and 42; John 9:1-7).

You Are Here

Quarterback Johnny Manziel was a first-round pick in the NFL draft. He was unstoppable in college, but after two years in the League his career ended. The reason? Even though he was highly talented, he was seriously immature. Johnny did not possess the self-awareness to evaluate his own life. The urgent quality a great teammate needs is the willingness to learn how to objectively look into his own life for strengths and weaknesses. It's called maturity.

Your life is like the Maps App on your phone that shows all the great places you want to go. But you haven't been there yet, so you need the map. Most importantly, you need that pinpoint that says, "You Are Here!" That's what a good parent, teacher, or coach does—shows you where you are so you can get to where you want to go. How mature are you as a teammate? How about as a Christian?

The Bible says, "Examine yourselves to see whether you are in the faith." (2 Cor.13:5) Ask the Lord to help you. We can't get cut from God's team, but we can spend all our time on the sideline of His purpose! Which category fits your true impact?

- Servant—The servant loves and leads his teammates. He always does what's best for them. He inspires others and sets the standard for hard work, faithfulness and trust.

- Committed—This teammate feels an obligation to his teammates and can be trusted. Though not the leader a servant is he will go the extra mile to help teammates.

- Employee—He does enough to meet team standards but needs others to motivate him to do things with excellence. He has some concern for his teammates if he isn't too busy with his own stuff.

- Fence sitter—He is committed one day and not committed the next. His relationships are casual rather than intentional.

147

- Rebel—He pulls in the opposite direction from where the team is going always creating distraction and dysfunction.

Let the Holy Spirit be your Pindrop!

He Is the Answer

Sometimes questions are more about giving information than getting information. One of my favorite coaches of all time is Norman Joseph. Occasionally at practice or in the middle of games he would ask, "Are you kidding me?" He wasn't asking about being kidded. He was telling all of us to wake up and get our heads in the game! My Mom would often ask me, "What were you thinking!" She wasn't interested in what I was thinking. She was saying, in fact, I wasn't thinking.

When Jesus asked His disciples "Who do you say that I am?", he wasn't fishing for a description of Himself. He was putting before them the question that all of history turns on. Simon Peter got it right— "You are the Christ, the Son of the living God." (Matthew 16:16) "Christ" means the One and Only, the Messiah, the One true God. The One that all of creation listens for! Here are more urgent questions from Jesus for you and me:

1. "What are you seeking." (John 3:8) What do you want in life? At the heart level, what is important to you?

2. "Are you offended." (John 6:61) Do you carry offense toward any person or group of people? As long as you stay offended, we won't get your best.

3. "What do you want me to do for you." (Matthew 22:18)3. What are your real motives?

4. "Do you understand what I have done for you?" (John 13:12) Humility and gratefulness are your greatest attributes.

5. "Why are you afraid." (Matthew 8:26) You can't defeat a fear unless you can identify it.

That one question rises to the top of the urgent questions of Jesus— "Who do you say that I am." (Matthew 16:15) Sooner or later we will all be held accountable for our answer.

Belonging

When I was a little kid growing up in Mississippi, most any adult in my town felt free to hug me or discipline me, whichever they deemed I needed, all without my parents' immediate consent. There was a level of trust and an element of family that was bigger than any one household. I'm sure there were sad exceptions where kids were abused. But as for me and my brothers, all we got was love, both the tender kind and the tough kind.

If you touch a kid today in any way who isn't yours you might be threatened with a lawsuit and jail, at the very least a suspicious look. It's so sad. I want all our children to be safe from abuse, but they also need to know the intimacy and care of the greater community.

From my experience with male athletes, the number one thing missing from their lives is a broad spectrum of healthy relationships with healthy adults.

One of my best friends growing up was Ronnie Walker. His dad was Coach Wade Walker, the head football coach at Mississippi State University. Ronnie and I stole some football game programs one time and sold them before the game for 100% profit! He found out about it and immediately whipped our young butts. He didn't call my parents or the police. He just laid into us. I can promise you we never made that mistake again and I'm grateful for him.

I had no doubt that Coach Walker loved me enough to send me a tough message! My last memory of him before he passed was the hug he gave me and the words of affirmation he spoke over my life. I can share dozens of examples of other citizens of Starkville, Mississippi— parents and teachers and coaches and neighbors who spoke correction and love into my life at the right time.

Have people changed? Are adults different? What about kids? Has our cultural consciousness gotten contaminated by fear, racial strife, and political agendas? Families move into neighborhoods and live there for years never even knowing the people on their own street!

Children were a central part of Israel's culture, its worship, and its celebration. The whole nation took responsibility for their care, training, and correction. The one thing that connected them all was their faith in and love for God. But today, joining a church and joining a community are not the same thing. I have more questions than answers. The one thing I do know is that we are losing our kids from the family of Christ. Maybe we need more dialogue and prayer. I know I need more hope that we can break free of modern isolation and rediscover Christian community. Our kids' futures are at stake.

Slow Money

I hate it when my poor planning causes me to use an ATM machine. Being charged to use my own money is ridiculous, yet ATM owners make billions of dollars charging us for the convenience of 24-hour access to what is already ours. ATMs thrive because of what we need or think we need in the moment. In our culture, waiting has become increasingly intolerable. I can tell my wife that I need a lawnmower and in 30 seconds she can have it on the way to our doorstep!

I wonder how many of us are frustrated, angry, or bitter right now because God has left us waiting on something we asked Him for. I once prayed for a road-worthy used car for our family at a good price. I prayed about it, but I didn't wait. I soon bought a car that turned out to be money pit. I didn't give God any time to work.

Shortly after I made that purchase, I good friend offered to give me a car that was in way better shape than the clunker! When we are impatient in our waiting, the enemy of our souls will find a way to make us pay for what is already ours!

Remember, just because we are waiting doesn't mean God is. He is always at work on our behalf. Waiting is not doing nothing. It's being obedient to Him in every way possible while He moves on our behalf. Don't let Satan make you pay for what is already yours! Here's some great encouragement from God's word:

- "The Lord is not slow to fulfill his promise as some count slowness, but is patient toward you,..." (2 Peter 3:9)
- "Wait for the Lord; be strong, and let your heart take courage; wait for the Lord! (Psalm 27:14)

- "But if we hope for what we do not see, we wait for it with patience." (Romans 8:25)

*I mean no disrespect to ATM owners. They are not the problem.

Drifting

They are called "Rumble Strips" and most of us have experienced them. They are those annoying treads at the edge of highways that warn you when your car is drifting off the road. It's the sound of distraction or slumber that has saved thousands of lives! I never give them a thought until they have saved me and my car from a crash. Rumble Strips are not a comforting sound. They are a sudden annoyance that can send a shot of painful adrenaline through your body. But in our culture of distracted driving, many of us would have been injured or killed without them.

Have you noticed that the Lord uses Rumble Strips? We'll be flying along the road of our lives and get that annoying Rumble Strip sound from heaven! It might come from your spouse who says something like, "Your anger is hurting your relationship with our children." Or your doctor says, "Your blood pressure is up." Or maybe depression has started to haunt the fringes of your life but all you know to do is keep plowing ahead.

Maybe you heard Jesus say, "If you even look a woman in a lustful way, it's the same as if you actually had sex with her." Brrrrrumph! Driving demands our full attention, just like living for Jesus. Today may we heed His voice, no matter how annoying it might sound. ("And after the sound of the wind and earthquake there came a gentle whisper." 1 Kings 19:12)

I Was There

During my senior year in high school, our second game of the football season was against Louisville High School, one of the best teams in the state. Both Louisville and my team Starkville felt that a win would set the course for a banner season. After a hard-fought game, we pulled away in the final quarter and won it.

Walking off the field after that victory was a transcendent moment for us. We began to believe. We were waking up to the reality that we were a group of players destined for a special season. We didn't lose another game all that year while setting several school records. The win against Louisville was a momentum-changing moment that caused us to realize our potential.

Although the Bible is full of transcendent moments, a few truly great ones stand out for me. Because of the power of God's word, we get to live them today and benefit from their transformational impact:

1. Extraordinary faith—Abraham on Mt. Moriah, knife drawn, ready to sacrifice his only son.

2. Leadership faith—Moses at the burning bush receiving his commission to deliver his nation from slavery.

3. Loving faith—David facing a giant with nothing but his slingshot and a heart that burned for God.

4. Revelatory faith—Simon Peter, in a burst of spiritual clarity, recognizing who Jesus really was, the Son of God!

In the heat of life's battles, it's important to remember these transcendent moments—the season in which we gave our hearts to Christ, the time when our gifting got connected to God's purpose, and the moment we experienced God's presence and peace in the middle of our defeat. "You are the Christ!" Peter finally got it! (Matthew 16)

Every Word

I've read the Bible through a few times and parts of it many times. Yet, every time I go back to it, I see new things. A verse that I know well takes on a deeper meaning. If I take time to study a single word, I usually get something new. When that happens, I get a deeper understanding of the verses that it comes from. I like to read a whole book through over several days. Doing that I sometimes get the greater context of its words and verses that I could not have seen before. I'm gaining revelation most days not because I'm more spiritual than others but because I might be more desperate than others!

"Blessed are those who hunger and thirst for righteousness, for they shall be filled." (Matt. 5:6) That's it. You don't need a theology degree or years of Bible training. You only need to be hungry for God and He will feed you! Remember these ideas when you're reading the Bible:

1. God wants you to get it. (James 4:8)

2. Being aware of your own brokenness is what creates humility and hunger, both of which are essential in knowing God through His word. (Matt. 5:3)

3. Don't worry about what you can't understand. Run with any revelation you do get, even a tiny bit. (James 1:22)

4. Seek to know the God of the Bible and you will know the Bible of God. (John 5:39)

5. Learn from other Christians who have a track record of serving God and loving people. (Phil. 3:17)

Reading the Bible and is not the same as eating its bread and its fruit! "Man shall not live by bread alone, but every word that comes out of the mouth of God." (Matthew 4:4)

Drifting

I've kayaked many miles in the great oceans. Those mighty waters teach me something new every time I go out. Maybe the most important thing I've learned is that you are never sitting still in one place. You might stop paddling and the wind and waves may be minimal, but the tides and ocean currents are unseen forces always moving you. You are never sitting still!

If you don't stay alert to your preferred destination, you can drift off course for miles before you realize what's happening. Those unseen currents never stop though it may appear that you have. It's the same in your spiritual life. If you're not moving toward the Lord and His purposes for your life, you're not sitting still. You are drifting!

Remember, if you don't have a destination, you're going somewhere! But when we are alert to the movements of the Spirit, we can easily catch the wind of His purposes.

157

Remember, He wants us to find our way! "For this reason we must pay much closer attention to what we have heard, so that we do not drift away from it." (Hebrews 2:1) Ask the Lord to set your course. Every day.

1. Psalm 32:8—"I will instruct you and teach you in the way you should go; I will counsel you with my eye upon you."

2. Psalm 37:23-24—"The steps of a man are established by the Lord, when he delights in his way; though he fall, he shall not be cast headlong, for the Lord upholds his hand."

3. Jeremiah 29:11—"For I know the plans I have for you, declares the Lord, plans for welfare and not for evil, to give you a future and a hope."

4. Isaiah 43:16-19—"Thus says the Lord, who makes a way in the sea, a path in the mighty waters, who brings forth chariot and horse, army and warrior; they lie down, they cannot rise, they are extinguished, quenched like a wick: "Remember not the former things, nor consider the things of old. Behold, I am doing a new thing; now it springs forth, do you not perceive it? I will make a way in the wilderness and rivers in the desert."

Hating on Hate

I can celebrate you without celebrating your values. I hope that I would give my life for your life, but please don't ask me to give it for your beliefs. What if I called you a hater because you didn't believe in Jesus Christ like I do? He didn't die an ugly death because He was a hater. He died because He was Truth. His words cut so deeply that they found the darkness of heart we all carry.

Yes, I celebrate you and all the greatness and beauty you carry. But if your lifestyle is contradictory to God's heart and design, love demands that I not remain silent. Truth expects me to take a stand for you. Can you honestly call that hate?

We cannot have freedom if we are free to do anything we want to do. That would be anarchy. By nature, freedom presupposes our commitment and loyalty to our laws and to one another. Likewise, we are responsible for raising our kids to be free. Dad and Mom, for the sake of freedom, your kids need you to hold them accountable. Here are 7 ways I see parents making their kids irresponsible people:

1. Give them unlimited choices.
2. Tolerate laziness in them by not teaching them to work and not making them work at home without pay.
3. Prevent teachers, coaches, and policemen from holding them accountable for their actions.
4. Tell them they can do anything and be anything.
5. Allow them to make their phone and their room off limits to you.
6. Tolerate meanness in them and a lack of empathy toward people and animals.
7. Allow them to disrespect anybody, especially you.

These things are guaranteed to rob your child's freedom making them dysfunctional, arrogant, and unhappy. Do you need to make some changes? Let's work together to set them free through responsibility, accountability, and compassion. If we are faithful in that duty, they will know the truth!

War Hero

It wasn't until the 1990s that Zofia and Andrzej Pilecki found out their father was a hero. As teens in postwar Poland, they had been told the opposite, that he was a traitor and an enemy of the state. They listened to news reports about his 1948 trial and execution on the school radio. But in truth, Witold Pilecki was a Polish resistance fighter who voluntarily got himself arrested by the Nazis and sent to the horrible Nazi prison called Auschwitz. There he started an historic resistance movement.

From behind those prison walls and barbed wire, Witold Pilecki sent secret messages to the Allies, becoming the first person to sound the alarm about the true nature of Nazi Germany's largest concentration camp. Despite extraordinary circumstances of starvation and violence at Auschwitz, Pilecki built a powerful and effective resistance movement that eventually led to freedom for all of

Germany's prisoners of war! Though a prisoner himself, he guided the entire WW II allied resistance movement!

All Witold ever did was help save people and they killed him for it. Sound familiar? Jesus infiltrated enemy territory as a resistance fighter to free people from the prison of their own sin. All He ever did was heal and save people. Like Witold Pilecki He built a powerful resistance movement, the purpose of which was freedom for all who would join Him. What a beautiful gift it is to give something you can't keep anyway for something that you can keep forever! Jesus, the War Hero of all time!

He Be Crazy

I met Henry on the beach yesterday. He is a handsome, intelligent, and sensitive guy who looked to be around 40 years of age. When I asked him if I could buy him some food, he said what he really needed was a pack of cigarettes. I gave him a 20-dollar bill and he immediately started digging in his pockets. He came out with an old bolt and snuff can full of matches. Then took his cap off and gave it to me as well—everything he had except the clothes off his back.

He randomly made comments about the Illuminati and how he couldn't open the door because someone was hiding and the drive-through is not real so don't go there. Like one in five Americans, Henry is suffering from mental illness. Many factors can lead to mental illness, including genetics, physical illness or injury, and traumatic life experiences.

Due to the associated stigma, only 44% of adults with diagnosable mental illnesses receive treatment. (USC School of social work) Sadly in our culture if you get labeled "crazy" it can become a life sentence. What about you? Have you ever experienced a time in your life that you felt you were going to "lose it"? Most of us have. Maybe not on the level of Henry's sickness, but we too experience overwhelming periods in which the pressures of life are crushing us. Our sense of well-being, our ability to enjoy life and meaningfully connect with others become broken.

If you or someone you know is suffering, no amount of money should stand in the way of getting help from mental health professionals. Find a counselor or therapist. Encourage your church to get equipped to help those of us who are willing to be honest about our true state of mind. As Henry and I parted yesterday he said as clear as a bell, "Bill, I really like you. Thank you." He's in there somewhere. I hope one of us can find him.

One Family, Many Races

Mankind was meant to be one family of many races, not one race of many families. As long as we prioritize race over family, we will remain broken. God isn't colorblind. Each of us was fearfully and wonderfully made by His loving hand. He made no mistakes when He gave us our skin color. Nevertheless, at the Garden of Eden, there was one family. Adam and Eve weren't a race, they were a son and daughter of their loving Father.

But then they went their own way. They wanted to self-determine who they were at the expense of connection with their good Father, at the expense of family. That arrogant self-determination continued in their descendants who tried to build a city and a tower called Babel, a monument to themselves. Instead of one family, mankind became many races separated and identified by rebellion more than color.

But God didn't quit on us. He brought man back to His family table through one covenant after another. His love didn't stop us. We continued to identify with race instead of grace. In Jesus Christ, the Father offered the final and most beautiful gift to us that we might be one Kingdom family forever.

We the people have made a mess of family because we have preferred race. We have allowed the Accuser of the

Brethren to separate us from the household of faith so he can destroy us outside the courtyard of our Father's house. We are living in fear and insecurity like orphans. We can't see the greatness in one another, only the differences.

How does our focus become one family of many races instead of my race of many families? Instead of responding with reasons we are divided, would you consider responding with ideas that will help us be united? Before you do, please read these verses that prioritize family over race:

1. "God shows no partiality, but in every nation anyone who fears him and does what is right is acceptable to him." (Acts 10:34-35)

2. "Have we not all one Father? Has not one God created us? Why then are we faithless to one another, profaning the covenant of our fathers?" (Malachi 2:10)

3. "And they sang a new song (to the Savior Jesus Christ) saying, 'Worthy are you to take the scroll and to open its seals, for you were slain, and by your blood you ransomed people for God from every tribe and language and people and nation, and you have made them a kingdom and priests to our God, and they shall reign on the earth.'" (Revelation 5:9-10)

Blaming God

Romans 8:28 is misquoted and misapplied quite often. God does not cause all things. He causes all things to work together for good for people who are demonstrating a desire to follow Him! And even for those who aren't pursuing Him, He is relentlessly pursuing them! The Father has proven throughout all history that He has never given up on reaching every single person on earth with His great love and purpose.

God doesn't need to cause a calamity. Humans are great at that without Him! And when you say, "He allowed this time happen" what exactly do you mean? Would you allow your child to get run over by a car because he was too immature to avoid that danger? You do everything you can to train and teach him about danger, over and over. God is always loving us and teaching us but are we listening? I'll tell you what God allows. He allows love and love demands freedom of choice.

"So, choose life in order that you may live, you and your descendants." (Deut. 30:19)

Romans 7:19 "For the good that I want, I do not do, but I practice the very evil that I do not want." (Romans 7:19)

"This is the judgment, that the Light has come into the world, and men loved the darkness rather than the Light, for their deeds were evil." (John 3:19)

"The person who sins will die. The son will not bear the punishment for the father's iniquity, nor will the father bear the punishment for the son's iniquity; the righteousness of the righteous will be upon himself, and the wickedness of the wicked will be upon himself."

(Ezekiel 18:20)

"For by your words you will be justified, and by your words you will be condemned." (Matthew 12:37)

IDENTITY

But you are A CHOSEN RACE, A ROYAL PREIESTHOOD, A HOLY NATION, A PEOPLE FOR GOD'S OWN POSSESSION, so that you may proclame the excellencies of Him who has called you out of darkness into His marvelous light; for you once were NOT A PEOPLE, but now you are THE PEOPLE OF GOD; you had NOT RECEIVED MERCY, but now you have RECEIVED MERCY." (1 Peter 2:9-11)

My son John Paul and me

Like My Father

How you define God will define you. The greatest revelation of Him is Jesus Christ who is defined as love, kindness, tenderness, majestic, mighty, holy, full of grace and mercy. In the light of His identity who then are you? Stop calling yourself a sinner, unlovable, unholy. Look on the Lord and see what He sees in you. Because of Christ's sacrifice, I find it necessary to remind myself of who I really am by using these "I am" declarations from God's word:

1. I am beautiful. ("I will give thanks to You, for I am fearfully and wonderfully made; Wonderful are Your works, And my soul knows it very well. Psalm 139:14)

2. I am a son and heir of the Father. "and if children, heirs also, heirs of God and fellow heirs with Christ, if indeed we suffer with *Him* so that we may also be glorified with *Him*. Romans 8:17)

3. I am a saint, majestic in nature, completely righteous. ("He made Him who knew no sin *to be* sin on our behalf, so that we might become the righteousness of God in Him. (2 Cor. 5:21)

4. I am the salt of the earth. "You are the salt of the earth; but if the salt has become tasteless, how can it be made salty *again?* It is no longer good for anything, except to be thrown out and trampled under foot by men." (Matthew 5:13)

5. <u>I am the light of the world</u>. "You are the light of the world. A city set on a hill cannot be hidden; nor does *anyone* light a lamp and put it under a basket, but on the lampstand, and it gives light to all who are in the house. Let your light shine before men in such a way that they may see your good works, and glorify your Father who is in heaven. (Matthew 5:14-16)

6. <u>I am more than a conqueror</u>. "But in all these things we overwhelmingly conquer through Him who loved us. For I am convinced that neither death, nor life, nor angels, nor principalities, nor things present, nor things to come, nor powers, nor height, nor depth, nor any other created thing, will be able to separate us from the love of God, which is in Christ Jesus our Lord. (Romans 8:37-39)

7. <u>I am "a chosen people</u>, a royal priesthood, a holy nation, God's special possession." (1 Peter 2:9)

Knowing my true nature in Christ doesn't make me arrogant or lazy, it makes me humble and confident that I can do anything He calls me to do! Confidence in my identity gives me confidence to help you discover your identity!

Crowbait

In the 6th game of the 1986 World Series, Boston Red Sox first baseman Bill Buckner let an easy ground ball roll through his legs allowing the New York Mets to score and win the game. If Buckner had caught the ball the Sox would have won the series, but instead the Mets won the 7th game and captured the crown! Buckner's mistake haunted him for the rest of his life. Boston fans heaped so much abuse on him and his family that he quit baseball and moved to Idaho. He never outlived the loser label.

I know a woman who was told at an early age that she was sexy. She has suffered much pain in her life because of that label. When I was a young kid, a coach gave me the nickname "Crowbait". I don't even know what that means but I know it shamed me. Sometimes I still find myself trying to outrun that label.

Labels can be very obvious but also implied—"Jim is just not a good student." The dirty work of labels is that they limit. They limit ability, promise, and aid. "That's just the way Sarah is. Let's try to love her anyway." Label. You need to know how God labels you.

- You are forgiven. (Eph. 1:7-8)
- You are secure. (Romans 8: 31-39)
- You are capable. (Phil. 4:13)
- You are valuable to God. (1 Cor. 6:20)
- You are dearly loved. (Col. 3:12)

How about wearing these labels and helping others to wear them!

Still Champs

University of Florida basketball coach Billy Donovan took his National Champion team on a weekend getaway before the following season started. He wanted to expose a dangerous threat to his team. People everywhere were asking his players, "As defending champions, can you win it again this year?" Coach Donovan wisely recognized that the label "defending champions" was not only dangerous to his team but was inaccurate. He told his players, "We aren't the defending champions, we are the champions! We can't go into the season in a defending mode. If we are true to who we already are, everything else will take care of itself."

That team made history by being the first to repeat as National Champions with the same 5 starters! What an incredible feat! The one thing that marked those Florida players was a calm confidence in the face of every battle. They remembered who they were and played from their true identities!

As sons or daughters of God, we can't get caught up in trying to win what has already been won. Nobody can rob you of your identity in Christ or the crown that will be yours in heaven. No person, nation, nor any enemy on earth can take what is yours in Christ. You were a champion for Christ yesterday and you will be a champion for Him today. Spend your energy on offense, taking territory for God out of your true identity in Him.

Heart in the Race

Secretariat was possibly the greatest racehorse of all time! On his way to stardom, he won the first 2 races of the Triple Crown (horseracing's National Championship). In the final race, even before the halfway mark, Secretariat had gained a huge lead. But instead of safely coasting to victory, he maintained a record setting pace, winning by 31 lengths! That would be like a 100-meter runner winning by 20 meters! Unheard of!

Years later after this champion horse died, his owner had his heart examined by a veterinarian. No wonder he was kicking butt! They discovered that Secretariat's heart weighed 2 ½ times more than the average racehorse! God had given him an extraordinary heart for an extraordinary purpose, the same thing He did with you and me!

David says in Psalm 119:32—"I shall run the way of your commandments, Lord, for you will enlarge my heart!" Amazing! Here are more incredible verses about the power of a great heart:

8. Our hearts are owned by whatever we value most. "For where your treasure is, there your heart will be also" (Matt 6:21)

9. Wisdom, understanding, and purity don't come from effort but from hearts that surrender to God. "Trust in the LORD with all your heart and lean not on your own understanding." (Proverbs 3:5; Psalm 51:10)

10. The condition of your heart effects every area of your life. "Above all else, guard your heart, for everything you do flows from it." (Proverbs 4:23)

11. The peace of God is the environment of healthy hearts. "And the peace of God, which transcends all understanding, will guard your hearts and your minds in Christ Jesus." (Phil. 4:7)

12. Our hearts get healthy when we allow God to examine them. "Test me, LORD, and try me, examine my heart and my mind." (Psalm 26:20)

13. If your heart is broken, only God can heal it, but He is so willing! "The LORD is close to the brokenhearted and saves those who are crushed in spirit." (Psalm 34:18)

14. "Blessed are the pure in heart, for they will see God." (Matt. 5:8) WOW!

Generational Blessings

My three children are all much better people and parents than I was. I can either feel threatened by that or rejoice in it. Looking back, I can see how broken my parenting was and still is! Trying to do the best I can with what I have just isn't always enough. My parents were like me. They gave their best to us but some of the old broken ways they had learned from the previous generation became my way of life. The Lord has much Good News about His people navigating the generations.

1. The threat of generational curses ended with Christ. In the New Covenant children are not held accountable for their parents' sin. (Jeremiah 31:29) The sin and mistakes of previous generations can negatively impact us but no longer have authority over us. (Exodus 20:5; Luke 22:20)

2. The number one priority of our generation is to testify of God's great heart, His wonderful acts to the coming generations. (Psalm 145:4; Psalm 78)

3. We are responsible for building a spiritual foundation for the coming generations. Whatever we build will cause them joy or grief. (I Peter 2:5)

4. We must find our New Covenant voices for the sake of the next generation. God has an anointing for each of us to speak with an authority that transcends culture. (Deuteronomy 32:7)

5. We are called to be darkness-penetrating intercessors for the next generation, proclaiming before all heaven and hell that they will love and serve the only true God. "But you are a chosen race, a royal priesthood, a holy nation, a people for his own possession, that you may proclaim the excellencies of him who called you out of darkness into his marvelous light." (I Peter 2:9)

The next generation is our responsibility. Let's pray for them, serve them, give them opportunities, and protect them. They are so worth it!

Discovery and Recovery

I saw a family get rescued from the roof of their home during a hurricane. Their gratitude was a beautiful thing to see as they hugged those who came for them. Jesus spent most of His life rescuing people. He demonstrated that rescue is the heart of God and the primary focus of the Gospel. It doesn't take any compassion to ask someone if they want to be saved. It takes a lot of compassion (and effort) to rescue someone. What God's word says about rescue:

1. Jesus rescued people by increasing their wealth. (John 2:1-11; Luke 5:1-11).

2. He rescued people with mental health problems. (Mark 1:23-28; Matthew 8:28-34).

3. He created lasting legacy by changing the entire direction of peoples' lives. (Luke 7:11-18).

4. He rescued people who were affected by major weather events. (Matthew 8:23-27).

5. He gave people new economic futures. (Matthew 9:32-33).

6. He rescued the hungry. (Matthew 14:15-21).

When you step out in faith to rescue someone, you can be sure that the Lord will back you with all kinds of resources to get the job done. Let's preach and live the Full Gospel— helping people **discover** Christ and walking with them as they **recover** from their lostness.

Note: Wisdom dictates that there are certain people at certain times who need to experience their adversity and lack. Before I met Christ, I floundered for several years keeping my family on the edge of poverty. Nobody came and rescued me. I needed to get in touch with the pain in my life so that I could surrender to God's great care. Let's help people but let's stay prayed up so that we can be led by Holy Spirit's great wisdom.

Entitlement

When I was the chaplain for a college football team, I got to work with the incoming freshmen. I learned that there was only one thing that could lead to them not making it—a sense of entitlement. If they were bigger than the program, they either left or never reached their full potential. That consumer attitude got started through parents and family when those young men were just little kids. Sport can be an incredible teacher for life with the right leadership. Here are 5 things for parents to remember about sports and kids:

1. Being rejected or overlooked is not a bad thing. It's one way God leads your kid to his/her true identity and purpose. Draw close to them in it but don't interrupt the process. Hard knocks fuel the fire of passion!

2. Help your kids learn the balance between wholehearted effort and fun. The beauty of competition is what it demands from them through blood, sweat, and tears. When you remove pain, you cut the heart out of sports. Yet, if they aren't having fun in it, help them understand why.

3. Preach and teach "teammates first". Train them up to be encouragers and supporters instead of consumers. A great question to ask after every practice/game, "How did you help a teammate?"

4. Let the coach or a teammate be the bad guy. Be the safe place for your kid to cry, laugh, and process.

5. If you care more about the sport than your kid does, then you are in danger of acting completely out of character. Sports is just one thing of many things your kid will experience in life. Let it simply be a growing and learning experience instead of preparation for "The Next Step" in their sports career.

One of the most important decisions my Dad ever made was to not interfere with my coach's authority and leadership. If I complained to Dad about a coach, his response was always the same—"Take it up with Coach. Praying for you. Let me know how it goes."

INTIMACY

"This is eternal life, that they may know You, the only true God, and Jesus Christ whom You have sent." (John 27:3)

Enid Lake Mississippi

He Calls Us

I remember the moment Mary Parker Buckley first spoke my name. We were standing in the doorway of her college dorm at the end of a date night after we had been seeing one another for a few months. As we discussed the meaning of our relationship she said, "When you get ready for something real Bill Buckley, you let me know." Wow! That statement held both challenge and invitation! It was a sobering moment for an immature college kid. But bigger than my fear was the resolve I experienced when I heard her speak my name!

Fear is the cause of our worst decisions. I cannot imagine walking away from her love if fear had had its way! What was I afraid of? Commitment? Failure? Inadequacy? Can you name your fear? How can you confront it and overcome it if you can't name it? Listen to what our Father says about it—"Don't fear, for I have redeemed you; I have called you by name; you are Mine." (Isaiah 43:1) How beautiful is that?! He called my name! When I have the confidence of God's redemption and nearness, no fear can live in me. I'm learning to confront my fear, to hear the Father's voice saying, "When you get ready for something real Bill Buckley, you let me know!"

Meditate on these Scriptures that speak of God's adoring love for you—

"But now thus says the Lord, he who created you, O Jacob, he who formed you, O Israel: "Fear not, for I have redeemed you; I have called you by name, you are mine." (Isaiah 43:1)

"Why, even the hairs of your head are all numbered. Fear not; you are of more value than many sparrows." (Luke 12:7)

"To him the gatekeeper opens. The sheep hear his voice, and he calls his own sheep by name and leads them out." John 10:3)

"Nevertheless, do not rejoice in this, that the spirits are subject to you, but rejoice that your names are written in heaven." (Luke 10:20)

It's Who You Know

I thought I knew Mary Parker when we got married. I had become familiar with her favorite foods, her clothing style, and musical talent. But as we started our life together, I began to learn about her on a whole other level. I learned what inspired her and what saddened her. I discovered what offended her and what made her feel valued. It's one thing to know a person's acts but a whole other thing to know their ways. The one is superficial, the other intimate. Spending time with someone and doing life with them are different universes!

What is true in marriage is true in faith. I can know about God and still not know His ways. I can read in the Bible about how He responded to people and not know why He responded that way. Psalm 103:7 says, "He (God) made known His ways to Moses, His acts to the sons of Israel." How was Moses different from the people he led? The people were pursuing a promise. Moses was pursuing a Presence! I don't love God or Mary because of what they can give me but because of who they are! These verses may help you better understand the Ways of God:

Isaiah 55:8-9—"For my thoughts are not your thoughts, neither are your ways my ways, declares the Lord. For as the heavens are higher than the earth, so are my ways higher than your ways and my thoughts than your thoughts."

Proverbs 3:5-6—"Trust in the Lord with all your heart, and do not lean on your own understanding. In all your ways acknowledge him, and he will make straight your paths".

Romans 12:2—"Do not be conformed to this world, but be transformed by the renewal of your mind, that by testing you may discern what is the will of God, what is good and acceptable and perfect."

John 14:6—"Jesus said to him, "I am the way, and the truth, and the life. No one comes to the Father except through me."

The Power of Pursuit

It was our first date, and we went to a quiet little cafe for dinner. We talked about nothing important while gauging one another like we all did in the college dating game. I didn't go back to my dorm room that night and tell my roommate, "Hey, I think I found the one." But I did wake up the next morning with her on my mind.

To be cool, I waited a few days before I dialed her up again. After that second date, something quietly shifted in me, something I had never experienced before. It wasn't the hot passion of youth but a dawning awareness I had never known. I couldn't have articulated it then, but looking back, I went from knowing Mary Parker to pursuing her.

A year later we would marry and decades later we are still in love. What has made the difference? It's that word "pursue". It changes everything. In its holy form, it's not about chasing after someone for sex or pride or fun. It's about discovering someone's heart. It means learning and valuing who they really are at the deepest level. Pursuit is so important that when it stops, marriages begin to die. Relationships dry up.

Maybe this is the reason that God talks about pursuit in the very beginning of His message to humankind. We read of Adam and Eve—"The man said, 'This is now bone of my bones and flesh of my flesh; she shall be called 'woman,' for she was taken out of man.' That is why a man leaves his father and mother and cleaves to his wife, and they become one flesh." (Genesis 2:23-24) The word "cleave" here means "pursue".

Men, are you still pursuing your wife? What does that look like for you? For me it's intentional, consistent, and Spirit-led before it becomes spontaneous. Ask God to turn on the pursuit mode in your heart so that you can go after your wife like you did when you met, hopefully now with the wisdom and kindness of maturity. Tell that offense you have against her to go to hell! Most importantly, when we move from knowing God to pursuing Him, we will automatically desire to do the same thing with our wives!

True Love Wins!

I grew up in a culture where men were conditioned to show no weakness and no emotions. That environment made me a solid athlete but a sorry man. My work ethic was strong, I could overcome adversity, and I knew how to fight. The one thing I didn't know how to do was love.

I have been discovering some things though—The Greatest Lover of all time also happens to be the Greatest Warrior of all time! His name is Jesus Christ and He defines real love this way, "YOU SHALL LOVE THE LORD YOUR GOD WITH ALL YOUR HEART, AND WITH ALL YOUR SOUL, AND WITH ALL YOUR MIND.' This is the great and foremost commandment. The second is like it, 'YOU SHALL LOVE YOUR NEIGHBOR AS YOURSELF." (Matthew 22:36-39) Pretty simple but not easy.

Love God. Right relationship with the Author of love is not about being perfect but being positioned. It's about being surrendered under the influence and power of His great heart. In His will is the most confident place I can be. Because He will never quit on me, I have the strength to never quit on you!

Love your spouse (who is your nearest neighbor). By protecting them in their weakness instead of attacking them. The grace God gives us empowers us to protect hearts without compromising our values. My wife sometimes covers a weakness in me until I am strong enough in faith to confront it. When I feel safe around her, she gets the full gift of who I am!

Love yourself. Not a selfish love but a healthy love that has the confidence to recognize and appreciate the strong qualities that God gave you. The key to finding greatness in others is recognizing it in yourself!

When these 3 relationships are right, everything else in your life will have to bow the knee to Love. Love that is a Person, Jesus Christ. He was no weakling. He fought the greatest battles in history and won them all by always doing what was best for all of us.

The One Who Sees

Mary Buckley knows where I am every minute of every day. Her phone has an app that shows her a map pinpointing my exact location. I travel some crazy places hiking and kayaking. She watches me because she loves me not because she's suspicious of me. But she's not the only one watching.

Last year I got a ticket for running a red light in California. (I swear it was still yellow!) I never had an encounter with a law officer, only a letter in the mail. We are on camera in most public buildings that we enter or sporting events we attend. And, of course, there are the Chinese and the Russians that many people claim are watching us in a wide range of ways.

Surveillance is big business in our day. Satan, your number one enemy, can't read your mind but he does have you under surveillance. I Peter 5:8-9 says that he is "always looking" for a way to exploit you and put you under his control. But there is One Who watches the watchers! Here are some of our good Father's promises about His watch care over His children:

1. "I am with you and will watch over you wherever you go, and I will bring you back to this (promise) land. I will not leave you until I have done what I have promised you." (Genesis 28:15, my parentheses)

2. "I will instruct you and teach you in the way you should go; I will counsel you with my loving eye on you." (Psalm 32:8)

3. "For the eyes of the LORD range throughout the earth to strengthen those whose hearts are fully committed to him." (2 Chronicles 16:9)

4. "For the eyes of the Lord are on the righteous, and his ears are open to their prayer." (I Peter 3:12)

5. "He rules by His might forever; His eyes keep watch on the nations." (Psalm 66:7)

Be at peace! The Lord has already seen your day and gone ahead of you in it! He will never leave you!

The Fountain of Youth

I'm old but my marriage is not old. Mary and I are best friends, madly in love, and co-laboring for the Gospel of Christ. For the children of God, eternity is a present reality, the fountain of youth from which we live our lives. Love doesn't grow old and anything is possible! Together we are new every morning. Great is God's faithfulness! May you and I continue to position our lives before Him in ways that transform all things. Here is what that has looked like for us:

1. We still pursue God and one another.

2. We have always valued people in our lives who love us and speak the truth to us.

3. We study God's word and give Him time to speak to us every day.

4. We've learned how to forgive.

5. We are intentional about serving others.

6. We believe our jobs and God's purpose are the same thing.

7. We never sleep on our anger toward one another.

Newlyweds in the kingdom. Because of our hope in the Lord.

"Therefore a man shall leave his father and his mother and hold fast to his wife, and they shall become one flesh." (Genesis 2:243)

"Let marriage be held in honor among all, and let the marriage bed be undefiled, for God will judge the sexually immoral and adulterous." (Hebrews 13:4)

"He who finds a wife finds a good thing and obtains favor from the Lord." (Proverb 18:22)

"Love is patient and kind; love does not envy or boast; it is not arrogant or rude. It does not insist on its own way; it is not irritable or resentful; it does not rejoice at wrongdoing, but rejoices with the truth. Love bears all things, believes all things, hopes all things, endures all things." (I Cor. 13:4-7)

Full Attention

My wife will not allow my phone to be a greater priority than her. If she is talking and I even glance at it, she will stop in mid-sentence and not continue until I refocus on her. She doesn't glare at me, pout, or scold me. She just disconnects from me, like I did her. She's not mean-spirited, she just wants the best of me and the best of her. Because she doesn't give me any angry words or attitudes, I have no recourse but to walk away frustrated or repent and give her my full attention. It helps me feel like an idiot for treating my wife like that which is a positive outcome that I can only blame myself for. Full attention. Hardly anybody these days gives it or gets it. Let's be different! "Give your entire attention to what God is doing right now.". (Matt. 6:34) Here are 7 ways to better give yourself to others in conversation:

1. **Silence Your Devices** – Nothing distracts like noise. Eliminate those alerts from your email, watch, everything!

2. **Close Your Screens** –Close that laptop. Shut off that monitor. And turn your phone face-down or put it in your purse/pocket.

3. **Don't Multi-task** –You are unable to give you full attention to more than one thing at a time. Nobody wants to talk to someone who is always spinning the plates.

4. **Face the Person You Are Speaking With** – Looking at someone face-to-face is a powerful way to demonstrate your attention. It builds trust and stronger communication.

5. **Listen Before Speaking** – Giving your attention doesn't mean that you have to jump to respond and provide answers to everything that someone is telling you. Listen *more* than you speak. Some of the best conversations occur when you *only* listen.

6. **Don't Let Interruptions Interrupt** – You think that interruption will only take a moment, but then the person you were talking to ends up sitting awkwardly while you address something else.

7. **Repeat What You Heard** – Nothing says "I heard you and understand," more than a polite rephrasing of what you have been told. It shouldn't

be robotic or patronizing, but a genuine repeating of what you have understood from the conversation.

God and Galaxies

There are 100 billion stars in our galaxy! The average distance between them is 30 trillion miles. Can you even spell "trillion"? There are over 100 billion galaxies in the universe! (What's your street address again?) The DNA information in one amoeba, the smallest living thing, would fill 1000 complete sets of the Encyclopedia Britannica!

Whether you go big or go small, the complexity and precision of life on earth is astounding! That life is detectable scientific evidence for the creation of the universe by an extraordinary Designer. It takes far more faith to believe that the universe somehow just happened than it does to believe that a loving Master Creator was at work. It is good to remember that "chance" is only a word not a cause and that this magnificent God is attentive to your heart every single day! Listen to what He says about Himself!

1. "He stretches out the north over the void and hangs the earth on nothing." (Job 26:7)

2. "By faith we understand that the universe was created by the word of God, so that what is seen was not made out of things that are visible." (Hebrews 11:3)

3. "The heavens declare the glory of God, and the sky above proclaims his handiwork. Day to day pours out speech, and night to night reveals knowledge". (Psalm 19:1-2)

4. "He determines the number of the stars; he gives to all of them their names". (Psalm 147:4)

Phenomenal love!

Love Corrects

I feared my 7th grade math teacher, not because she was mean or angry, but because she possessed a fierce, sometimes mysterious determination to make me better. If you tried to sneak some laziness or bad attitude into her classroom, it was only a matter of time before you found yourself standing alone before her. Yet, I never witnessed her get angry or impatient. Quite the opposite, she was resolute regarding rules but kind in enforcing them.

Though she was unwavering in her judgments, she was never unfair, and when you had suffered her discipline, she would always bring you close, speaking words of encouragement and challenge. Interestingly, when I walked away from her after those corrective encounters, I always felt lighter, better, cleaner. Mrs. Eckhart demonstrated the quality of leadership of our Lord. Psalm 19:9 explains it best—"The fear of the LORD is clean, enduring forever, the judgments of the LORD are true, they are righteous altogether." Fear of the Lord is not condemning. It's cleansing and purifying. Before Him we don't cower. We bow! There's nothing like feeling clean!

"Therefore, since we have these promises, dear friends, let us purify ourselves from everything that contaminates body and spirit, perfecting holiness out of reverence for God." (2Cor. 7:1)

"Create in me a pure heart, O God, and renew a steadfast spirit within me. Have mercy on me, O God, according to your unfailing love; according to your great compassion, blot out my transgressions. Wash away all my iniquity and cleanse me from my sin. (Ps. 51:1-3)

"If we confess our sins, he is faithful and just and will forgive us our sins and purify us from all unrighteousness." (I John 1:9)

War Lord

Many of us have been taught about the kingdom of God but few about the kingdom of darkness. Americans appear to know very little about Satan and his army of demons. Maybe it's because they know that our culture will laugh at you if you believe in God but think you should be locked up if you believe in Satan.

Most of the "photos" we have of Jesus show Him to be a passive, sweet little man who wouldn't harm a flea. But He was no common civilian suffering the attacks and harassment of Satan. He was the Pioneer and Captain of our salvation, the original Soldier of the cross. Satan cannot touch the finished work of Calvary, but he can prevent you and I from taking ground for the kingdom already won.

It's time to take our position in "the heavenly places" beside our Commanding Officer. We are no longer free to play the role of civilians, living as if there is no war. The history of believers in every age is one of conflict. It's time we learned who the real enemy is. It's time we stopped fighting people and people groups, political agendas, and human philosophies. It's time we learned to fight the real war in the spirit realm. Here are some questions soldiers of the Cross must answer:

1. Does my life express the hostility God put between Satan and Jesus? What does that look like? What does that mean for me today?

2. Are there any ways in which I am seeking coexistence with Satan through compromise?

3. Is my conviction about Christ and His purposes strong enough that others readily see it? Is my faith radical enough to be public?

4. Have I made myself available to the Lord for warfare training? Do I know what it means to submit to God and resist the devil?

5. Have I heard from God about a specific territory of darkness that is my assignment to conquer?

My brothers and sisters, the war is on! Ask God for your place in His army!

Sex is Good

Our sexuality holds extraordinary power. It can be used to comfort or control, to help us discover our identity or cause us to lose it. It has the capacity to create beauty or rob our souls of everything beautiful, to leave us completely satisfied or always hungry. Whether married or single, young or old, a person of faith or an atheist, you possess the power and beauty of sexuality.

Jesus was never married but his sexuality was alive and well. "For we do not have a high priest (Jesus) who is unable to sympathize with our weaknesses, but one who in every respect has been tempted as we are, yet without sin." (Hebrews 4:15)

Stewarding your sexuality is a life-long wonder. How beautiful is the testimony of 2 virgins consummating their marriage! It is a glory for a prostitute to fall in love with Jesus and be pure in a moment! What transformational power between husband and wife when unfaithfulness loses to forgiveness and restoration! You don't get to determine your sex. You get to steward it before the Lord with honesty and obedience.

No Place to Hide

I wish every kid could spend 3 years under Coach Jim Craig. He was my high school football coach and in those 3 years we lost only 2 games and won 2 conference titles. Coach Craig was a winner. Here are some things he taught me about football and life:

1. We value you but it's not about you, it's about us.
2. You will be held accountable for your actions and attitudes on and off the field.

3. There's no place to hide here so you better come out fighting.

4. Relentless effort always outlasts talent. Be relentless or be gone!

5. We respect your parents, but they have no say here.

Coach Craig taught us to be personally accountable, a deep well I draw from every day! He made us champions because he's a champion! Moms and Dads don't interfere with your kid's teachers and coaches. Let them fight their own battles and take responsibility for their own failures and successes. You are critical to their development but not responsible for their success! One of the best things my dad ever told me was, "You need to take that up with Coach Craig. Let me know how it goes."

"For we must all appear before the judgment seat of Christ, so that each one may be recompensed for his deeds in the body, according to what he has done, whether good or bad." (2 Cor. 5:10)

"For each one will bear his own load." (Galatians 6:5)

Behind the Scenes

College football equipment managers are the closest thing to the true Christian life. Seriously! Everything they do is for somebody else. On Friday they load big trucks with uniforms, shoulder pads, helmets, shoes, headsets, and footballs for about 60 players and 10 coaches. The same day they hit the road to somewhere like Gainesville, FL, nine hours and 538 miles away from somewhere like Mississippi State U.

At the stadium they unload everything, putting each player's and coach's gear in the visiting locker room, setting up the sideline with headsets, extra gear, and footballs. Their work is often frantic during the game with issues like getting a key player back on the field after equipment failure. Sometimes the game is on the equipment manager's shoulders! Yet if they get on camera, it's only by accident!

An hour after the game, with cameras flashing and autographs being signed, players and coaches are escorted to the airport for a quick trip home. The equipment managers stay behind in the smelly dressing room to load up EVERYTHING and start the long drive back to campus. For a 6:30pm Saturday game in Gainesville, FL they get back to MSU around 10:00am on Sunday.

These amazing people unload everything, wash uniforms, and maybe get a nap before starting another relentless week! They are rarely noticed until something breaks or is missing. They don't get bonuses or interviews. Yet, they do their job every week, making everything else work for everybody else! They are the backbone!

Equipment managers represent our calling in the kingdom of God—people who are willing to do sweaty jobs unnoticed with a selfless, relentless attitude. Our job is to do whatever it takes to get everything ready for Jesus to get the spotlight! Your greatest accomplishment today might go completely unnoticed by everyone but Him! Make sure everyone around you has everything they need to succeed! Whatever it takes. When nobody is watching!

Pain and Gain

I remember a particular game when I was coaching high school basketball. We lost in triple overtime to our biggest rival. Our kids played so hard that it broke my heart to look at their faces as we huddled at our bench. We were all crushed. At the time, none of us knew that would become our defining moment. Those kids could have folded and coasted for the rest of the season. They didn't! We went on to become conference champions, finishing with the best record in school history!

The pain of that triple overtime loss forged something in our hearts. A powerful conviction rose up in those guys from the suffering of defeat. I'm reminded of Jesus and His defining moment. The Scriptures tell us, "When the days were approaching for Jesus to be crucified and to be risen from the dead, He 'set His face' to go to Jerusalem." (Luke 9:51) Sold out. That's what happened. Being sold out to the Father's will carries us safely through all defeat and, sooner or later leads to victory! Set your face to go all the way! If you will not give in, hardship will reveal the overcomer in you!

When you get beat, write out these Bible verses and post them on the dashboard of your car.

"The LORD is my light and my salvation; Whom shall I fear? The LORD is the defense of my life;

Whom shall I dread?" (Psalm 27:1)

"Blessed is a man who perseveres under trial; for once he has been approved, he will receive the crown of life which *the Lord* has promised to those who love Him." (James 1:12)

Translation—I'm not quitting!

Family Ties

I know Mary Parker Buckley. Not only have I lived with her my whole adult life, but I have studied her, pleased her, angered her, and repented to her! I have loved her and feared her in the same moment! I have both listened to hear and ignored her, but I have never quit trying to understand her. John 17 is the most beautiful prayer in history, spoken by Jesus to the Father. In it He says, "This is eternal life, that they may know You, the only true God, and Jesus Christ whom You have sent." (Vs.3) That word "know" means "to understand at the deepest level".

I know a lot of people, but the list of people whom I understand is small indeed! You can't say you know Jesus without possessing an understanding of His great heart and mind. It takes your whole heart to really understand somebody! I could not know Mary if I hadn't been in her presence learning about her! Let's pursue the Lord with everything we've got so that our understanding of Him keeps growing. He is so ready for you!

Most people I meet don't have a family. Oh, they might be living with some folks who carry their DNA, but their lives are dysfunctional and directionless. God created family from the beginning and from the beginning it has been under attack. Are you still broken because of your family of origin? Be encouraged! The Lord is able to create family around you! Here are 7 things a family should be giving:

1. Identity—recognition and proclamation of your authentic God-given gifting.

2. Stability—a structured and supportive place to grow.

3. Belonging—confidence that you are welcomed and loved.

4. Health—provision for physical, emotional, and relational wholeness.

5. Safety—an environment of peace and security.

6. Truth—education and cultivation of personal purpose and destiny.

7. Honor—recognition and respect for your position in the family.

The message of the Gospel is a good Father bringing sons and daughters into His family through His Son! When the family gets healed the world can get healed!

LEADERSHIP

"Where there is no guidance the people fall, but in abundance of counselors there is victory." (Proverb 11:14)

Father of Waters, the Mighty Mississippi River

God's Man

Today, men are being treated like puberty-stricken adolescents. You might say, "Well, that's the way men act." I'm sure many of us are acting immature, but I believe there are bigger reasons. In the American cultural arena, maleness must fit obediently into political sensitivities and media-filled expectations. Men can't be too loud, and they can't be too quiet. We can't be macho but we surely can't be soft. We are expected to appear powerful but not be powerful.

I hear coaches say today's boys get their feelings hurt too easily, while women say men are weak because they aren't in touch with their feelings! Many of us really do want to be a part of the empowerment and success of the women in our lives. But many women don't believe men are in any way a part of their growth process.

I've attended one Men's Retreat after another, all of them calling out men to be men, defining what a real man is and doing "real man" things. But we will never know who we are by looking between our legs! The reason so many of us can't control our sexuality is because of the pressure we experience in trying to be something we were never created to be.

Our maleness has gotten highjacked by an antichrist movement bent on destroying our truest purpose. Look for yourself. There is no manhood emphasis in the New Covenant in Christ. We didn't get born-again so we could be our true masculine selves. In Christ, we are beloved sons of a good Father. A man who knows how to be a son will know how to be a brother and a father. From the strength and wealth of that relationship, we get to be part of the great and beautiful Family of God!

We died to self in Christ not to become men but to become servants, Kingdom Men if you will. I'm surely glad I don't have to prove my manhood to you or anybody else. The mandate of my life is not to be a man, but to leave everything and follow Jesus. If I do that first, I believe I will find manhood in the process. My Brothers, be on the alert, stand firm in the faith, act like men, demonstrate manhood by being a good son of a good, good Father, faithful and true!

Note—Don't take 1 Corinthians 16:13-14 out of context.

Royal Correction

Tony Dungy was a head coach in the NFL for 13 seasons. His teams were perennial postseason contenders. He led the Indianapolis Colts to victory in Super Bowl 41. The guy could coach! When he first started working towards becoming a head coach, people wondered if he could do it.

He wasn't the type to yell at players or get in their faces. Many didn't think he could control his teams. Boy did he prove them wrong!

Coach Dungy's coaching style provides a great example of the difference between correcting and criticizing. He relied on consistent motivation, first-class instruction, and timely encouragement. The rules were nonnegotiable, and punishment was clear. When a player did something wrong, the goal was to help him become a better player and a better person. What is the difference in correcting and criticizing? Here are the dictionary definitions—

1. Criticize—to point out faults in a disapproving way.
2. Correct—to adjust to function accurately or in accord with a standard.

Criticizing focuses on mistakes and weaknesses while correction focuses on proper function and improvement. Criticizing often carries the components of frustration and anger. Correction is authority under control through timely and patient discipline.

Jesus made people think by asking questions and pointing out truth in unlikely places. The only thing he ever condemned was arrogance. Whether you are a coach or a parent or an employer, if you want the best from those you lead, work toward consistent motivation, first-class instruction, and timely encouragement. We're all better for it. "Fathers (leaders) do not exasperate your children (those you lead); instead, bring them up in the training and instruction of the Lord." (Ephesians 6:4, my parentheses)

Worst-Moment Love

During a National Championship Basketball game, Georgetown player Fred Brown had the ball with 6 seconds left as his team trailed by one point. Just enough time was left to run one play. James Worthy, a North Carolina player, suddenly darted toward the backcourt and Fred, mistaking him for one of his own teammates, threw the ball right into his hands. A surprised Worthy dribbled the clock out and North Carolina won!

Georgetown Coach John Thompson immediately ran to Fred Brown who had just made the biggest mistake of his life. Grabbing Fred in a big embrace Coach Thompson said, "Let's go home Fred! We'll be back in this game and you are going to lead us. Let's go get ready." Two years later, John Thompson's prediction came true. Georgetown was back in the title game and Fred Brown led his team to a great victory. In the worst moment of his life, Fred Brown had someone in his corner who was secure enough and mature enough to help him overcome his failure.

John Thompson is like our good Father. When we make mistakes, He doesn't sling a water bottle across the courts of heaven or roll His eyes or give us the silent treatment. He spontaneously runs to us and embraces us. His message is the same, "My son, my daughter, let's go back home and figure this out together." There will be someone in your life soon who will need you in their worst moment. Get ready now. Study the Lord's great heart. Don't be afraid of other peoples' failures. Like John Thompson, you may have only one golden moment. Make it count!

Overrated

I mean no disrespect to other Christian leaders, but we are mostly overrated. Do you think that because I can write popular media posts or preach a so-called "strong message" or hold a position of "Christian leadership" that I am closer to God than others? I am grateful for any place of influence, but I claim no special spirituality or authority.

My goal in life is not to be a role model for you but to be a catalyst for you. If the way I live my life emboldens you in your faith in Christ, I have served you well. If my words and actions make you comfortable where you are, then both of us need to repent. Remember our brother Stephen? His preaching was with such conviction that the people listening put their hands to their ears so they could no longer hear his piercing words. Then they ran at him and stoned him to death! So much for seeker-friendly messages. (Acts 7)

The only quality I possess that matters eternally is the desire to change and grow through the revelation of Jesus Christ in me. If my deposit in you does not have that capacity, it was only words. "But encourage one
another day after day, as long as it is *still* called "Today," so that none of you will be hardened by the deceitfulness of sin. (Hebrews 13:3)

Pecan Pie IQ

Did you know that genius Albert Einstein was a lowly patent clerk before he became the most famous scientist in history? Patent clerks review patent applications to determine whether the proposed invention should be granted a patent or whether the application should instead be refused. It was from that quaint patent office that he first submitted to the scientific community his theory of relativity, possibly the most astounding discovery in scientific history. Because he was a complete unknown who was working at a menial job, no one in the scientific community took him seriously. It was years before other scientists recognized the significance of Einstein's discovery.

I believe everyone has some genius in them because we were all created in the image of the Genius of the universe! Part of the job description for every follower of Jesus is to discover their own genius and help others discover theirs'.

I know a man whose life work is pecans. He was one of the first people to learn how to graft trees, that is, grow better pecans on a tree that's producing poor ones. That doesn't sound like much compared to the theory of relativity, but that man has helped thousands of Southerners make an income growing pecans!

Have you ever considered your own genius? It may not have anything to do with your current job. What about the genius of your kids or grandkids? Genius is not about grade point average but rather the Creator's deposit! You have genius in you! Maybe that genius is that you were designed to live an uncommon life with very common intellect and skills, like me! Allowing Christ to live through us, now that's genius, like Einstein!

"But if some of the branches were broken off, and you, although a wild olive shoot, were grafted in among the others and now share in the nourishing root of the olive tree, so do not be arrogant toward the branches. If you are, remember it is not you who support the root, but the root that supports you." (Romans 11:17-18)

Pacesetter

Mom and Dad, are you going at the speed of your family? The 20th century was a time of unmatched change in our nation as we moved from an agricultural economy to an industrial economy. The pace of rural life gave way to the hectic pace of company mandates, quotas, and deadlines. We were able to buy more, go more, and want more. We moved from a contemplative people to a multi-tasking people.

Remember that old church song about the Lord, "He's got the whole world in His hands"? Well, now you and I got the whole world in our hands! It's called a mobile phone! The problem is not the technology. The real threat is allowing the technology to get the best of your life, it's the possibility of losing our souls and our families in the crush of culture.

But this is not a new problem. Centuries ago, a man named Jacob got a job change and was moving his family. He wisely saw the weight of his decision on his family. His response was brave and clear—"My children are small and weak as are my cattle and sheep are. If they are driven hard, they will not survive. Please allow me to travel at their pace." (Genesis 33:13-14)

Moms and Dads, are you going at the speed of your family? What is a healthy pace for you and them? Let's pray for one another, pray for clarity about how our work habits and schedules are impacting our families and our own souls. May God give you the grace to live your life at His pace for you and your family. Ask Him about it. He has a plan. I don't want you to have to deal with the regrets I carry because I couldn't say no to the expectations of others at the expense of my wife and children.

Plan To Win

Our football team had a Plan To Win—four essential things we had to get done to position ourselves for victory. Every week we preached, promoted, and lived it. The Plan To Win is amazingly accurate as a guide for faith and life as well. Check it out!

1. Play great defense. Our priority is to defend and serve our family, our coaches, and teammates (our church). ("Be devoted to one another in brotherly love; give preference to one another in honor."— Rom 12:10)

2. Win the turnover battle. Get the ball. Go get your stuff back, stuff that gets stolen by the enemy like hope, confidence, courage, and identity. Your stuff

is your responsibility! Go get it back! ("Then David recovered everything that the enemy had stolen—all the women, all the children, all the sheep and camels—not one thing was missing. David brought it all back."—I Samuel 30).

3. Red zone scoring. (When we reach the other team's 20 yard line, we have to come away with points.) The team that recognizes opportunity will usually win. Don't get distracted by things you can't control and miss once-in-a-lifetime moments. ("So then let us not sleep as others do, but let us be alert and sober."—I Thess. 5:6.)

4. Special teams. Be a role player. Be willing to take the highest place or the lowest place, whichever helps your family, church, or team the most. This may be the biggest key to victory. We win only when everyone knows his assignment and completes it. ("He who is faithful in a very little thing is faithful also in much."—Luke 16:10)

Amazing how this plan can help us win in football games and in life! What is your Plan To Win?

Learners Win

In 1982, Howard Schultz took a job serving up coffee at a small shop in Seattle. Three decades later he is the billionaire owner of Starbucks Coffee Shops, the largest coffee-shop chain in the world! If you looked only at Schultz's academic record, you would miss his genius. The quality that made him brilliant was not academic ability.

As a matter of fact, he was only a fair student in the classroom. Highly observant, connectible, and industrious Howard Schultz possessed the ability to learn from all the people he encountered in life. That sounds so simple but very few people possess this basic quality of a true learner—observing and processing life from someone else's perspective.

From my experience working with young people, I've learned that the primary thing they need is not money or educational opportunities. The first thing they need is close relationships with people who are achievers, people who have never quit learning. The most impactful teachers and coaches I ever had were all people who were on the move. You could feel the momentum of their lives by the way they related to others, by their selfless energy and passion. They weren't all about the win or the money.

True

I went to high school with a girl named Jean Ann Wofford. Of all the kids in our school, she stood out as someone with a true heart. She loved the Lord and showed kindness to us, her classmates. She wasn't perfect but her long-term genuineness is a beautiful thing. When many of us were living broken and rebellious lives, Jean Ann remained true to God. I didn't want to be anywhere around her, while at the same time, I wanted to be with her all the time! I was both convicted and drawn.

A true heart is the greatest transformational force on earth. It's the reflection of an inner beauty and power that can only come through wholehearted faith in Jesus, the One with the truest heart! Here's what the He says about "true":

1. "Blessed are the pure in heart, for they shall see God." (Mathew 5:8)

2. "Finally, brothers, whatever is true, whatever is honorable, whatever is just, whatever is pure, whatever is lovely, whatever is commendable, if there is any excellence, if there is anything worthy of praise, think about these things." (Phil. 4:8)

3. "The aim of our charge is love that issues from a pure heart and a good conscience and a sincere faith." (I Tim. 1:5)

4. "And everyone who thus hopes in (Jesus) purifies himself as He is pure." (1 John 3:3)

5. "He who speaks from himself seeks his own glory; but He who is seeking the glory of the One who sent Him, He is true, and there is no unrighteousness in Him." (John 7:18)

(For many years Jean Ann Foxworth and her husband Randell served as missionaries in the jungles of Papua New Guinea. Amazing!)

Get Out in It

I'm so grateful to Rupert and Sally Buckley, my amazing parents! When we were kids, every summer we traveled to some incredible state or national treasure, camping everywhere we went! We hiked to Clingman's Dome overlooking the Great Smoky Mountains. We camped in Yellowstone National Park and the Badlands of South Dakota. We caught trout in the Pecos Wilderness Area of northern New Mexico and broiled them on a riverbank fire! We hiked to the bottom of Carlsbad Caverns, the darkest place on earth! We swam in the glacier-fed waters of Jackson Lake at Jackson Hole, Wyoming.

Those were some of the most instructive, formative times of my life! We learned how to set up and take down a camp, how to start a fire, and safely traverse a mountain trail. We learned that the world was much bigger than us and that God was truly majestic! We came to understand there were National and State Treasures we all owned together.

Get your kids or grandkids out in nature. You don't have to spend a fortune and you don't have to travel far. Our state has some beautiful state parks and dozens of hiking trails. Getting out in nature is good for the heart, soul, and body! The outdoors creates a peace like no other and a closeness

to God you can't get in a building. Leave a nature legacy!
America the beautiful!

Blame Game

The number one thing God asks each one of us to do is to
take full responsibility for our own life. We don't get to
blame other people for where we are today. I have a heart
to help people struggling in poverty, but poverty will not go
away until the people in poverty learn to take responsibility
for their own lives. Maybe I can help them get there. Most
of us carry some hurt from the way other people treated us.
But we don't get to blame them. We get to take
responsibility before the Lord for our own healing.

There are all kinds of injustices that come our way every
day. It's part of life and that will never change until the
Lord comes back. I want to do everything I can to help you
in any way I can but when you start demanding that I do,
that only makes it harder for you to be helped. The most
loving thing I can do for you is to help you be personally
responsible for your own life. That is the one thing that will
lead to healing and wholeness. Here are some things God
says about it from the Bible:

6. "The one who is unwilling to work shall not eat" (2 Thessalonians 3:10).

7. "For each person must bear his own load." (Galatians 6:5)

8. "But if anyone does not provide for his relatives, and especially for members of his household, he has denied the faith and is worse than an unbeliever." (1 Tim. 5:8)

9. "Whatever you do, work at it with all of your heart for God and not people." (Col. 3:23)

10. Arise, for it is your task, and we are with you; be strong and do it." (Ezra 10:4)

11. "My mistakes are my responsibility." (Job 19:4, my paraphrase)

Core Values

Over the years my core values have changed in my pursuit of Jesus. My values describe where I spend the best of my time, talent, and treasure. Values give my life meaning and direction. What are yours? Maybe you could use mine to create your own.

Football Team Core Values

- Promote team. Put team goals above personal goals.

- Protect women. Treat women with respect.

- Practice honesty. Demand no lying, cheating, or stealing among your teammates.

- Pursue honor. Respect the authority of your parents, coaches, teachers, and the law.

- Prosper teammates. Take responsibility for the welfare and success of your teammates.

Personal Core Values

1. The Good News. I believe the gospel message is primarily an invitation, not a warning. (John 3:16; John 8:1-11; Matthew 6:10; Matt. 10:7)

2. Father's love. I believe God is a good, good Father calling sons and daughters home to His heart through the life of Jesus. (Rom.2:4, Rom.8:15; Gal. 6:4).

3. Family. I believe we are called to royal, covenant relationships instead of doctrinal agreement. (I Peter 2:9; 2 Cor.3:6)

4. Finding gold. I believe our number one purpose in relationships is relentless love that finds the beauty and greatness in people so they can confront the darkness in their lives. (Matt. 16:17-18; I Cor. 14:26)

5. Accountability. I believe in helping people be responsible before the Lord to steward their giftings and divine assignments. Accountability is "accounting for your abilities" more than telling someone else about their sins. (I Cor. 9:24; Eph. 4:29)

6. God is speaking. I believe God still speaks and without his present voice (by the Holy Spirit) we will have little understanding of His word, His purposes for our lives, or our place in history. (I Cor. 12:4-11; I Cor. 14:1)

7. Supernatural empowerment. I believe all followers of Jesus carry His love, character, and power and

that we were meant to bring the fulness of Him into all the earth. (Isaiah 9:7; Matt.3:2; John 14:12; 2 Tim.3:5)

LOVE

"Owe nothing to anyone except to love one another; for he who loves his neighbor has fulfilled the law." (Romans 13:8)

Goose Point Biloxi, Mississippi

Zero Tolerance

My teammate Mike Turnipseed was one of the best high school athletes I've ever known. He had speed, athleticism, and strength. Mike was smart, fun, and always seemed to be in a good mood. For all his friendly appeal, Mike did not tolerate lawlessness or half-heartedness in himself or his teammates.

His life revealed the urgent difference in unconditional love and unconditional tolerance. We can love someone fully and not tolerate their values and behavior, despite what our current culture demands. Mike showed us that it's not Christ-centered love to be OK with a friend's destructive decisions and behavior that bring shame and create pain. We can love someone deeply but openly confront wrong in their lives.

Listen to what a leader in Bible times said about it—"Now we command you, brethren, in the name of our Lord Jesus Christ, that you keep away from every brother who leads an unruly life and not according to the tradition which you received from us. If anyone does not obey our instruction in this letter, take special note of that person and do not associate with him, so that he will be put to shame. Yet do not regard him as an enemy but admonish him as a brother." (2 Thessalonians 3:6,14,15)

Speaking the truth in love seems to be a lost tradition. Are we either too harsh and critical or too accepting of the sin that destroys people and relationships? Lord help us to be led by kindness while remaining true to the convictions of Your heart, like Mike Turnipseed.

Hearing Is Believing

When my brothers and I were little kids, our grandfather would often hide things from us. Things like birthday presents and small amounts of money. The love and adventure we experienced searching out Pappy's treasures drew us to his heart. God's word tells us that it is the glory of the Lord to conceal a matter, but the glory of His sons and daughters to search out His mysteries. (Proverb 25:2) The Lord's intention as a good Father is not to hide things from us but rather to hide things for us.

We can get discouraged when we don't recognize the different ways in which He communicates His love with His people. Here are 7 of those ways:

1. Scriptures. Most of us can testify that we have had a word or a verse jump off the page as we were reading. The words come to life as we consider and meditate on what we are reading with a hungry heart. God will never violate His Word, but He will often violate our understanding of His Word! (2 Timothy 3:16-17).

2. God's still small voice. It's easy to underestimate the power of God's whispers. His still small voice can be heard as a passing thought or momentary impression highlighting the need to pause, to wait. (1 Kings 19:11-13)

3. Angels. Throughout the Bible angels appeared to people speaking instructions from God. (Luke 1:26ff)

4. Creation. The whole earth and universe speak daily of the greatness and power of God! (Psalm 19:1-2)

5. Impressions. All of us have probably experienced impressions in our spirit as we entered a room, a city, or the presence of a certain person. My spirit groans if I travel into certain parts of New Orleans. The darkness becomes oppressive.

6. Circumstances. Sometimes we view difficult experiences as if we have deviated from God's plan. But if you are going after God and His purposes, Satan will be on our tail! Don't let Him distract you from what God is doing and saying. (John 10:10ff)

7. Visions. Visions occur when the Lord stirs our imagination with images and pictures. Most often, this is how the Holy Spirit speaks to us. Visions often appear like pictures that require interpretation. (Acts 2:17-18)

The most important question anyone could ask you—"Have you heard from God this week?"

Offense—Opiate of the Soul

Have you ever met anyone who never got offended? No, because offense is in the DNA of every human soul. This powerful state of mind and heart holds the power to destroy relationships and take lives. It's no small thing, so we need to stay alert to how it operates and what we can do as followers of Jesus to limit its destructive impact.

Below is a brief Bible study of what God says about offense. Read and meditate on these verses: Proverb 19:11; Matthew. 5:38-42; Luke 17:3-4; Ephesians 4:2-3; Proverb 27:5-6; James 1:19-20; 2 Timothy 2:24; 2 Corinthians 13:11; Romans 12:17-21; John 13:34-35. Here are some lessons I've learned the hard way about offense:

1. You can't stay offended at somebody you genuinely love. Love demands that you give your best to that person but offense will never allow it.

2. Offense has a very quiet shelf-life. You may have forgotten you are offended until the perfect storm of circumstance and people and then all hell can break loose, damaging relationships with the people you care for most.

3. If you don't make your own offense your own responsibility you will stay offended your whole life.

4. Unforgiveness is the proper name for offense. Call it what it is.

5. Offense waits to show itself until the worst possible moment to create the worst possible damage.

6. A real being is behind offense—Satan himself. This is no small battle.

7. Offense is one of God's ways of purifying your heart. Give Him access. Surrender your offense to Him and you will grow exponentially!

Love Does

It was the biggest moment of 13-year-old Natalie Gilbert's life. She was singing the National Anthem before a nationally televised National Basketball Association Portland Trailblazers Game. About halfway through the song, fear came over her face as she suddenly forgot the words. In that moment, Portland Trailblazers head coach Maurice Cheeks walked over to her, put his arm around her and started singing where she left off. Natalie immediately regained her composure and finished beautifully! Coach Cheeks could have easily let that extraordinary moment slip by, but he didn't hesitate to come to the aid of someone struggling in the limelight.

That incident inspires a question for all of us—Are we becoming a "walk by" culture in which we conveniently ignore the needs and problems of people we don't know? From the homeless man on your street corner to the stressed-out mom trying to get her kids and grocery bags into her car, is the pace of our culture making it easier to walk on the other side of the street?

Everybody you meet today is fighting a hard battle. Before you walk out your door, ask the Lord for the compassion and courage you'll need for small acts of kindness that carry the power to change a day and even a life! It's the second greatest commandment—love you neighbor in his time of need. Your neighbor isn't the one who lives next door to you but the one who is standing next to you! (Luke 10:25-37) Be ready! Be a Maurice Cheeks!

Sideline View

As a football player, coach, and sports ministry guy, I have seen much on the sideline. Even though surrounded by your teammates, coaches, and fans, it can turn out to be a very lonely place. Fumble the ball, drop a pass, or miss a field goal and that sideline space can become a wilderness. I've had former teammates tell me their football experience was the loneliest time of their lives. I remember a player fumbling the ball and costing a big win. Fans tormented him so badly the following week that he left school and never came back. Surrounded by hundreds of classmates, his loneliness became unbearable. Sadly, he's still haunted by that experience.

Loneliness is not about being alone. It's being separated from belonging—the acceptance, the kindness, and the encouragement of others. Loneliness is no respecter of persons and doesn't care whether you are rich or poor, young or old. Can you recognize loneliness in your own life? It can look a lot like self-pity, cockiness, busy-ness, or even anger. You can put a smile or a smirk on it. You can try to fool yourself in a hundred poisonous ways so you don't feel it, but it can remain in your soul like a microchip volcano!

Loneliness is so important that it is one of the first things God dealt with in the beginning of Creation. He said to the universe, "It's not good for the man to be alone." (Genesis 2:18) Satan also knew the power of loneliness. He successfully separated man from the only place on earth where loneliness is not possible—the presence of God.

But in Christ, we got brought back from the loneliness of lostness! The solution to your loneliness problem is only one God-encounter away! I believe that Jesus experienced loneliness for our sake. It's why He needed the wilderness, the mountains, and Gethsemane, so we would never forget that His loneliness was our redemption! (Luke 4:42)

Sons and Daughters

I watched a 12-year-old foster child being presented a birthday present by her foster dad. As this young girl opened it, she began to weep uncontrollably. The gift was a certificate of adoption! This meant she would never go back into the foster system but would forever be this man's daughter! It was so beautiful to see her heart breaking in all the right places. From that moment on she wouldn't only take up a bedroom, she would take up his name!

What a beautiful picture of what God has done for us. The Bible says, "But those who embraced Him (Jesus) and took hold of his name were given authority to become the children of God!" (John 1:12) When you surrender to Jesus, you leave the orphan life forever by laying hold of His name. That means to believe all that He represents and to live out all that He taught in the power of His name. It doesn't get any better than being a son or a daughter of the living God! It doesn't matter who you are, God the Father is holding your adoption papers waiting for you to walk away from your orphan life! If you've never surrendered your life to Him, let it be today!

"He defends the cause of the fatherless and the widow, and loves the foreigner residing among you, giving them food and clothing." (Deut. 10:18)

"Religion that God our Father accepts as pure and faultless is this: to look after orphans and widows in their distress and to keep oneself from being polluted by the world." (James 1:27)

"A father to the fatherless, a defender of widows, is God in his holy dwelling. God sets the lonely in families..." (Psalm 69:5-6)

"In love he predestined us to be adopted as his sons through Jesus Christ, in accordance with his pleasure and will . . . " (Ephesians 1:5)

The Devil Made Me Do It

Have you been taught about the kingdom of God but not about the kingdom of darkness? What do you know about Satan and his army of demons? In our culture people might laugh at you if you believe in God but want to see you locked up if you believe in Satan. Most of the "photos" we have of Jesus show Him to be a passive, frail man who wouldn't harm a flea. But He was no common civilian suffering the attacks and harassment of Satan. He was the pioneer and Captain of our salvation, the original soldier of the cross.

Satan cannot touch the finished work of Calvary, but he can prevent you and I from taking ground for the kingdom already won. It's time to take our position in "the heavenly places" beside our Commanding Officer. We are no longer free to play the role of civilians, living as if there is no war. The history of believers in every age is one of conflict. It's time we learned who the real enemy is. It's time we stopped fighting people and people groups, political agendas and human philosophies. It's time we learned to fight the real war in the spirit realm.

Does your life express the hostility God put between Satan and Jesus? What does that look like? What does that mean for you today? Are there any ways in which you are seeking coexistence with Satan through compromise? Is your conviction about Christ and His purposes strong enough that others readily see it? My brothers and sisters, the war is on!

Doctrines Aren't Holy, God Is.

Can your Bible doctrines be saved?! I encourage you to take another look at your church's doctrines. They are more than likely true to God's word, but it is important to make certain that they are. Here are some thoughts about what doctrines are and what they can never be:

1. The word "doctrine" is used 9 times in the New Testament and simply means "teaching" or "instruction". The Bible never calls a doctrine inspired because doctrines do not possess the dynamic "living and active" power of Scripture. We

get into trouble when we try to make doctrines holy. "But in vain do they worship Me, teaching as doctrines the precepts of men." (Matthew 15:9, NASB)

2. Doctrines are like a road map that contains printed roads and highways that represent real roads and highways. It is possible for a manmade map to contain errors. It's the same with doctrines.

3. Like any teaching, doctrines can be helpful in gaining accurate revelation of the Living Word, Jesus Christ. But doctrines can never be more than a teaching, and teachings must always be open to correction by The Holy Spirit.

4. If your doctrines define you then somehow you have gotten disconnected from God's great heart.

5. It's the hungry babies that get truth! "Therefore, putting aside all malice and all deceit and hypocrisy and envy and all slander, like newborn babies, long for the pure milk of the word, so that by it you may grow in respect to salvation, if you have tasted the kindness of the Lord." (1 Peter 2:1-2)

Rebels With A Cause

I remember when I was in college my brother Paul and I drove from our home in Starkville, Mississippi to an epic venue called The Warehouse in New Orleans, LA. There we met with several hundred other faithful rebels and heard an amazing artist named Leon Russell. We left Starkville at 3:30 PM and returned at 7:30 AM, just in time for class! We were smoking marijuana all the way there and all the way back! Broken for sure, but you got to admit, we were sold out to our cause!

Going without sleep, food, or any basic necessities we were completely committed to who we were and what we were doing! Wouldn't it have been great if some local Christians had found the faith and imagination to help turn our crazy, radical hearts toward passion for Christ? I've often wondered if they were too intimidated or disgusted with us to attempt to such a thing—starting with the greatness and passion we carried instead of their 4 spiritual laws. Don't forget, crazy, radical people are only one decision away from doing crazy, radical things for the Lord!

America has always been a country of rebels. Our birth as a nation happened because some rebels stood up against the British. We broadened our borders because rebels took off into the Wild West! Rebels led the anti-slavery movement and the women's suffrage movement and the Civil Rights movement. Something in us gets inspired when we witness the edgy, risk-taking courage of a rebel. We need more rebels who are committed to compassion for people and love for God!

But there is a dark side to being a rebel that serves self by giving the finger to whatever is conventional just because you can. It is fueled by arrogance instead of kindness. If you will give the Lord access to your heart, he will not rob your wildness, he will empower it with purpose and honor! There is a difference in being in rebellion and being a rebel. "By faith Moses, when he had grown up, refused to be called the son of Pharaoh's daughter." (Hebrews 11:24)

I love how the message Bible translates Romans 2:9-19, a message about rebels—

"If you go against the grain, you get splinters, regardless of which neighborhood you're from, what your parents taught you, what schools you attended. But if you embrace the way God does things, there are wonderful payoffs, again without regard to where you are from or how you were brought up."

Confidence

Decades ago, before the LSU baseball team became a dominant national power, they found themselves in the SEC championship game. One more out and they would be SEC Champs for the first time ever. With two men on base and two outs in the bottom of the ninth, the batter hit an easy fly ball to LSU's right fielder. He dropped it. LSU lost and it was years later before they began to be consistent winners. When asked later about what should have been an easy out, the right fielder made a staggering comment—"I knew my teammates didn't believe I would catch it. I knew I would drop it."

Something was missing from that team. They had talent, coaching, and opportunity but they didn't believe in one another yet. There is a respect that must be earned through dedication and ability. But there is another kind of respect that believes in and honors others, no matter what. It's not conditional. It's not based on how good you are or how well you played. It's a gift. The Message Bible says, "God will never give up on you. Never forget that." (I Corinthians 1:8). When I am confident in God's unconditional respect for me, I get released to reach my greatest potential. Failure becomes opportunity. Weakness gets covered by His power and grace. Somebody needs you to believe in them today, no matter what!

"Each of you should use whatever gift you have received to serve others, as faithful stewards of God's grace in its various forms. If anyone speaks, they should do so as one who speaks the very words of God. If anyone serves, they should do so with the strength God provides, so that in all things God may be praised through Jesus Christ. To him be the glory and the power for ever and ever. Amen." (I Peter 4:10-11)

Closer Than A Brother

Mary and I spent two hours today with a husband and wife. They brought more healing and strength to us in that short time than we have known in many months. We were experiencing the weight of the normal pressures of life, family, and ministry. We felt lonely, overwhelmed, and tired. The spiritual and relational maturity of this couple was such a healing and energizing thing. They aren't professionals, just Christian friends. They loved us well, giving both correction and direction, always speaking the truth in love.

We've spent many years cultivating our relationship with them. We share a deep and rare level of trust. You cannot put a price on a relationship like that. I know many of you couples out there desperately need the kindness, compassion, and wisdom of someone outside your family, someone you can be completely honest with. Ask the Lord for help. Look around in your life for people who love the Lord, who demonstrate His heart. Invest the time to build a close relationship with them. Learn to trust. Mature, loving friends are 24 carat gold!

"A man of too many friends comes to ruin, But there is a friend who sticks closer than a brother." (Proverb 18:24)

"A friend loves at all times, And a brother is born for adversity." Proverb 17:17

"This is My commandment, that you love one another, just as I have loved you. Greater love has no one than this, that one lay down his life for his friends." (John 15:12-13)

"Oil and perfume make the heart glad, So a man's counsel is sweet to his friend.

Do not forsake your own friend or your father's friend, And do not go to your brother's house in the day of your calamity; Better is a neighbor who is near than a brother far away." (Proverb 27:9-10)

NEW LIFE

"And I will give them one heart, and put a new spirit within them. And I will take the heart of stone out of their flesh and give them a heart of flesh, that they may walk in My statutes and keep My ordinances and do them. Then they will be My people, and I shall be their God." (Ezekiel 11:19-20)

Gulf of Mexico, Long Beach. Mississippi

God-Sorry

One day I stood in front of a fire that was burning with all the illegal drugs, drug paraphernalia, books, and music that represented my life without God. I asked Him to forgive me and walked away from that flaming mess with nothing but resolve. I had tried to make changes in my life before, but this time was different, and the difference-maker was a thing called remorse.

Remorse is being so regretful of who you have become in word, deed, or lifestyle that your defenses are disabled, and your excuses quieted. All you can do is stand in the presence of Holy Justice and wait for instructions.

Remorse is the essential experience of entering into relationship with God and living in healthy alignment with Him and others. The most dangerous people on earth are not the most violent, law-breaking ones. No, they are people in your life like that respectable office mate you sit next to every day or the friendly waiter at your favorite restaurant. That gun-toting street thug may be seriously broken but brokenness can be healed.

The one thing God cannot heal is the person with no remorse. They are the covenant breakers and serial killers whose hearts have died on the vine. But not you! Not me! When we possess a deep and painful regret for wrongdoing and a wholehearted willingness to accept responsibility for that wrongdoing, all things become possible!

With good reason I've often wondered about those passages in the book of Revelation that describe hell as a place of eternal "weeping and gnashing of teeth". I believe those verses give us a vivid image of remorse when it comes too late! But it's not too late for me and you and the people in our lives!

"Peter remembered the word which Jesus had said, 'Before a rooster crows, you will deny Me three times.' And he went out and wept bitterly." (Matthew 26:75) Peter the coward became Peter the apostle. Remorse opened his life to God's heart in new and beautiful ways! For me, that fire of remorse so long ago became the fire of the Holy Spirit that still burns today! Remorse before the Lord always leads to freedom!

Dead or Alive

Lazarus, the man who Jesus raised from the dead, wasn't a little bit dead, he was completely dead, having been in a tomb for 4 days! In modern America we would have already had his funeral and put him six feet under! We know that Jesus was not only demonstrating His divine power by raising him up but was teaching us about what it means to be born again. "Jesus said to (Martha, Lazarus' friend), 'I am the resurrection and the life; he who believes in Me will live even if he dies, and everyone who lives and believes in Me will never die. Do you believe this?'" (John 11:25-26)

You can't be a little bit dead. You're either completely dead or totally alive, born again or altogether lost. Those who are truly born again have the Holy Spirit dwelling in them. (John 3:5) The work of the Spirit is to guide us into a living relationship with Christ. Here are four essential characteristics of a born-again follower of the Lord:

1. Conviction—an undeniable awakening to your lostness. (God's work)

2. Surrender—a bold decision to surrender to Christ. (Your responsibility)

3. Revelation—a growing awareness of the Person and works of God. (The Holy Spirit's influence)

4. Transformation—a new desire to pursue the Lord with your whole heart. (You and God together)

Before I met Christ I was completely dead! I'm not the best example of a Christian you've ever known but, like Lazarus, I know without a shadow of doubt that I believe in Christ and that I will live forever in His great Presence! I hope you have that confidence also.

The Bank of Decision

Mary and I were standing together on the bank of a very large lake many years ago. Only months earlier we had become Christians and were gradually coming to the realization that we owed God our whole lives. We were asking Him the question—"Lord, what do you want our lives to look like?" We were so green in the faith we didn't even know if that was the right question!

Ours wasn't a bold romantic faith, it was more like a blue-collar thing, the realization that we knew we must get something done for the Lord. I wish I could tell you it was a joyful moment, but it wasn't. It was one of the most sober times of our lives.

With all the faith we could find, we symbolically stepped off the bank into the Water of His Will.

We told God we were serious, and we needed to know the meaning of our lives as He defined them. We came up out of that lake with only a cold hard decision. We both had a scary, hopeful belief that our lives would always be like this— getting off the bank of convention and tradition into the living waters of God's unknown.

We've made so many mistakes and many wrong turns, but we have never regretted that moment. It was far more than "getting saved". We knew God had us. That moment has made all the difference in our lives, and we have never been the same!

What familiar bank are you standing on? Have you been there too long? Do you too need to step out into the great unknown of God? Life is short. It's time to get moving!

"Then he brought me back to the bank of the river. Now when I had returned, behold, on the bank of the river there *were* very many trees on the one side and on the other. Then he said to me, "These waters go out toward the eastern region and go down into the Arabah; then they go toward the sea, being made to flow into the sea, and the waters *of the sea* become fresh. It will come about that every living creature which swarms in every place where the river goes, will live." (Ezekiel 47:7-9)

White As Snow

One of your greatest challenges as a Christian is believing that you are completely innocent. Old lies and new mistakes want to make you sin-conscious instead of God-conscious. If you really believed you were completely pure, your heart would be so open to the Lord! The blood of Jesus covers our sin, frees us from condemnation, and makes us guiltless. But being exonerated is not hardly the whole truth about our innocence.

In the Lord, we could be living in a place of wonder—free from deception, unpretentious, and unsuspicious—like a little kid who has yet to be contaminated by adult agendas. When shame has your attention, you will always be looking for a fig leaf. But shame is not who you are! God chose you to be His very own, joining you to Himself even before He laid the foundation of the universe! (Ephesians 1:4) I wrote this poem about the emerging innocence between Mary and me:

Innocence

You were twenty I twenty-one
People said it couldn't be done.
No money for a ring
Nor money for anything.
We loved so hard we loved so raw
So much was wrong, but we saw
Each other's heart a world between
A hope for us beyond the seen.
Two girls a boy and then the years
Much pain and blood, sweat and tears.
We passed the quitting place in time
Like a mile-marker on a dime.
And felt some surge within our hearts
A mighty River run off the charts.
And lives that once uncertain flowed
Now sure and strong toward the unknown.
Our hearts they beat so strong as one
You are twenty, I twenty-one!

Bill Buckley 2017

Don't Feed the Bear

I read a story about a journalist who spent weeks in the wilderness documenting his encounters with nature. Soon, a bear was drawn to his camp by the smell of food, and one day the man gave the hungry animal a few scraps. Feeding the bear became a regular pattern as the writer was getting some fantastic photos. After the journalist failed to return home at the designated time, a search party went after him. All they found were bits and pieces of him and his clothing. The bear had killed and eaten him! Dang. The moral of the story? Don't feed the bear.

Every one of us is visited daily by a powerful and dangerous beast called "the natural man", that dangerous animal we were before we got transformed by new birth in Christ. We each have a choice to feed our new man or the old man, that old bear who consumes us and all that is good.

Paul said, "For I joyfully concur with the law of God in the inner man, but I see a different law in the members of my body, waging war against the law of my mind and making me a prisoner of the law of sin which is in my members." (Romans 7:22-23) When a culture begins to die, it never begins with the erosion of its values. The source of national confusion is not primarily about ignoring constitutions and laws. It comes down to one thing, feeding the bear, the unbroken human will. It's called rebellion against God, and it devours lives, families, and nations.

But when Jesus is allowed to rule our hearts, the bear can have no power. I don't know about you but today, no matter what else happens, I'm going to do my best to pursue Christ. I hope you will also. Don't feed the bear.

When Healing Hurts

I had a bicycle accident when I was 12 years old. Racing one of my buddies down a hill, I hit some loose gravel causing me to crash, sliding and tumbling for a while! Cut and scraped from head to toe, I limped back home wounded and broken. With four sons my mother was conditioned for this kind of thing.

She made me strip naked so she could examine my wounds. Then she cleaned them by bathing me in soapy hot water. Finally, she put plenty of Merthiolate on every cut and scrape. Remember Merthiolate? It was this fiery, red antiseptic that made you feel like someone was holding a branding iron to your skin! In truth, Mama's care was almost as painful as the accident! But through it all, her love for me was never in doubt and her healing ways kept me safe.

There was a time when I was racing full speed down the road of life. Because of my bad choices, I crashed hard. It was the loneliest and most painful time of my life. Little did I know that at the bottom of the hill of failure, God was waiting. He took me and cleaned me in the bath of Jesus' blood. He began touching all my wounds with His healing power. It hurt immensely, and at times I couldn't distinguish between my old wounds and His new touch. I had to come to a place of faith where I completely trusted Him with my pain.

Remember, the only time God hurts is when He is healing some wound in you or using you to heal the wounds in others. I pray that you can always find your way back home to His loving care. "Do not regard lightly the discipline of the Lord, nor faint when you are reproved by Him, for those whom the Lord loves He disciplines, and He scourges every son (and daughter) He receives." (Hebrews 12: 5-6) Sounds like Merthiolate to me!

Crowbait

When I was a 7th grade football player, I got the nickname "Crowbait" because I was so skinny and homely. If you're from the South, you probably know that a crow will eat most anything by picking over trash and leftovers. It was a hard name to carry, and I spent many years trying to outrun it. What I didn't know at the time was that the Lord allows the world to name us so we can be overcomers, and in the process discover His true name for us.

The book of Revelation is one of the scariest books in the Bible with its graphic end times descriptions of war and terror. This amazing book was not written to bring fear but faith. The term "overcomer" is especially prominent in its chapters where Jesus encourages His people to endure with faith through trials. (Revelation 2:26; 3:21; 21:7) I John 5:4-5 says, "For whatever is born of God overcomes the world; and this is the victory that has overcome the world—our faith in Christ." And Revelation 2:17 says, "To Him who overcomes I will give some of the hidden manna, and I will give him a white stone, and a new name written on the stone which no one knows but he who receives it."

Wow! Your true name is hidden in God's heart to be revealed as you fight the battles of your life. Your new name is true to your identity in Christ. It is accurate. It describes the greatness and beauty God put in you. What has the world tried to name you? Don't believe it! Overcomer. That's who you really are!

People Need the Lord

If we leave people like we found them we are not being true to God and His purpose in us. After you have met us, you should be more loved, more convicted, or maybe more comforted. You should have old questions answered and new questions emerging. It would be a shame if nothing happened because we carry the greatest transformational force on earth, not an impersonal force but a wonderful God, a mighty Counselor, Immanuel! His desire is that all people experience His radiant presence so they will know their true identity in Him and His amazing purpose for their lives.

Today, what part would the Lord have you play with each person you see? One sows and one grows, one reaps what was sown. (John 4:37) It won't look or sound the same for each of us. A smile, a warm greeting, or a helping hand are evangelism. I've seen so many misdirected opportunities and false conversions because well-meaning Christians shrunk their war chest down to the 4 spiritual laws and the sinner's prayer.

Make no mistake, if we are related to a non-believer long enough, love demands that we make him aware of his lostness. But from my experience, that is rarely the starting place. True evangelism is "love drawn out"—patient and forbearing, wise and unselfish. It's a marathon not a sprint.

Today, be aware of each person you meet. Ask the Lord what they need most. Be ready. Don't leave then like you found them!

Belief Deposit

A young man walked into the Army Recruiting Center and boldly signed up. As it turned out, he was only 16 years old. One of 6 children of an abusive, alcoholic parent, he did the only thing he knew to get away from a life of hell.

After discovering what the kid had done, his high school football coach talked the Army out of having him arrested for lying about his age. The coach then found him a home with a local family where he lived until he graduated high school. The kid earned a football scholarship, graduated college, and began a coaching career that lasted over 35 years!

When I was 16, unlike the kid, I had good parents and a good home life, but I too was living in a type of hell created by my own fears and insecurities. I wasn't looking for the Army Recruiting Center, but I was running hard from being abused every day through the lies I had come to believe about myself.

As an athlete, I was pretty much an "also-ran" until late in my junior year when something happened that changed the trajectory of my life. On the last day of spring football practice, one of my coaches walked with me from the practice field to our locker room. In those 5 minutes he told me I was going to be "a difference maker" on our team, to keep working, that he believed in me.

I went into summer workouts with a new fire in me and the following season was my best ever. Later, I would play college football and become a coach for many years. Oh, that coach who walked me off the field? His name is G.T. Thames, the 16-year-old kid who tried to join the army. What a powerful circle of influence! There are literally hundreds of us who owe him so much because of the influence he had on our futures. I share this not for your entertainment but for your participation. Stay alert for even a five-minute window with a kid who really needs encouraging in the most important moment of his life!

OVERCOMER

"For whatever is born of God overcomes the world; and this is the victory that has overcome the world--our faith." (I John 5:4)

Mississippi Sound Gulfport, Mississippi

The Last 10%

I remember an almost out-of-body experience I had in the fourth quarter of a high school football game. I was so exhausted that I could hardly think. The last 5 minutes of that very close game still seem like a dream. Later, when we viewed the game film, I realized those last 5 minutes were my team's best 5 minutes. The last 10% of everything my teammates and I had was what made victory possible. This is a powerful principal that works in all of life! Whether you are winning or losing, it's so easy to quit when you're running up on empty. But it's in those urgent moments that we demand our hearts to go where they've never been before.

Remember the last five minutes of Jesus's life? Voices were clamoring for him to come down off the cross. But he would have none of it! With the last 10% of everything He had, He gave you and me everything we needed for eternal life! Are you at 10%? "Be strong and do not give up, for your work will be rewarded." (2 Chronicles 15:7)

Sometimes when I want to quit, I have to stop and let the Lord recalibrate my heart. I don't know about you, but my heart wanders way more than my mind does! I have to make myself wait on the Lord by reading and digesting His Word. Especially words like I Corinthians 13. I am very convicted. Here is how I processed this powerful chapter. What if you read this chapter today and put it in your own words like I did?

1. No matter how much knowledge and information I possess, if I don't love people well, I'm only a loudmouth. (Vs. 1)

2. No matter what I tell you my cause is, if I am impatient and unkind, you will know my cause is me. Vs. 3-4)

3. Love means I can hear your heart above the sound of my own needs. (Vs. 5)

4. It is impossible to love if I remain offended. (Vs. 5)

5. Love is always grateful for the truth, even if it's personally painful. (Vs. 6)

6. Love believes in and works for the greatness in people, never quitting on them. (Vs. 7-8)

7. Love is the key to all wisdom and knowledge. (Vs. 8-10)

8. Love will always find our immaturities so that we can grow. (Vs. 11)

9. Love should be the number one priority of every follower of Jesus. (Vs. 13)

"Love is patient, love is kind *and* is not jealous; love does not brag and is not arrogant, does not act unbecomingly; it does not seek its own, is not provoked, does not take into account a wrong suffered, does not rejoice in unrighteousness, but rejoices with the truth; bears all things, believes all things, hopes all things, endures all things. Love never fails; but if there are gifts of prophecy, they will be done away; if there are tongues, they will cease; if there is knowledge, it will be done away. For we know in part and we prophesy in part; but when the perfect comes, the partial will be done away. When I was a child, I used to speak like a child, think like a child, reason like a child; when I became a man, I did away with childish things. For now we see in a mirror dimly, but then face to face; now I know in part, but then I will know fully just as I also have been fully known. But now faith, hope, love, abide these three; but the greatest of these is love." (I Corinthians 13:4-12)

Stay In the Fight

My son's very first week as a football player he got matched up one-on-one against the baddest, biggest kid in the league. John Paul was still wet behind the ears and this kid steam-rolled him! I was thinking to myself, "Well, that'll do it. Maybe he'll like another sport besides football." But he got right back up and got right back in the game. Years later as a high schooler he would become his team's MVP and one of the top players in the state. I was going to be proud of him either way, but I was especially proud because he stayed in that fight.

John Paul's life demonstrates an important truth—If it doesn't challenge you, it won't change you. He and his warrior wife Rachel are not afraid of a challenge! They moved from Mississippi to California with nothing but strong values, dreams, and love for one another and God. They have become champions as evidenced by the home they are building, the business they are thriving in, and the lives they are changing.

Has life hit you in the mouth? I doubt very much that God caused that, but He is in it with you to win it! Remember, He exploits the challenges of your life to bring transformational change in you, change that reveals the greatness already in your heart! His words for you today— "But as for you, be strong and do not give up, for your work will be rewarded." (2 Chronicles 15:7) "Surely the righteous will never be shaken; they will be remembered forever. They will have no fear of bad news; their hearts are steadfast, trusting in the LORD." (Psalm 112:6-7) "Be on the alert, stand firm in the faith, act like men, be strong." (I Cor. 16:13)

Fourth Quarter

Two-a-day football practice. In August. In Mississippi. Waking up at 5:30am, already tired and sore. Running drills in 95-degree heat until you can't breathe. Wanting water more than your girlfriend. Me and my teammates, those experiences shaped our lives. The longer we endured, the more confidence we gained. All that pain and suffering, it waited, it lasted. It became in us the staying power we would need to fight every play, to win the fourth quarter, to play our last game with the same passion as our first one.

Football taught us to "abide". That's a word you don't hear much today, but Jesus used it a lot. It means to sojourn with, to wait, to remain, to be continually held, to last, to endure. Here are some things the Lord says about abiding:

1. When we abide in the Lord, our junk starts dying and we get free to grow in pure faith. (John 12:24)

2. The key to loving others well is abiding—remaining, lasting, enduring beside them. (I Cor. 13:7)

3. Abiding creates the vision required to see a great and beautiful future on the other side of pain. (Hebrews 10:36)

4. Abiding is an active verb. It creates the patient, persevering strength we need to follow God's purposes for us. (Hebrews 12:7)

5. Abiding brings us into fullness, maturity, and completeness. (James 1:4)

"But those who wait for the LORD will gain new strength; They will mount up with wings like eagles, They will run and not get tired, They will walk and not become weary." (Isaiah 40:31)

Stay Hungry

I have many years of experience working with Mississippi Junior College football teams. Never have I witnessed a more talented, competitive football league! Mississippi Junior College Football is loaded with outstanding coaches and players. They are relentless. There's no soft place in the schedule.

What makes MS JUCO football so different? These extraordinary athletes are "hungry", desperate to win and be recognized by 4-year college football recruiters, desperate to prove they can play at the next level. Hunger may be the most important quality of an athlete or coach because, sooner or later, hungry will defeat talent and adversity.

Hunger is an internal reality, a condition of the heart. You can't teach or coach hunger. You can only discover it in yourself. All of us, we were born hungry—hungry for love and meaning in our lives. When you stop being hungry, you lose the ability to reach your greatest potential. It's hunger that drives us beyond what's comfortable, beyond average.

What do you have an appetite for? What really satisfies your life? Finding out what you are hungry for is one of the great keys to life. Being hungry only for material things is like having a diet of nothing but sweets. Being hungry for recognition is like eating nothing but bread—it might fill you up but it will never really satisfy you.

Ask God to stir up hunger in you, hunger for the things that matter in life! Hunger for Him! Hunger for making an eternal impact on those around you. "Blessed are those who hunger and thirst for righteousness, for they shall be satisfied." (Matthew 5:6) There's no satisfaction like the satisfaction of making an eternal difference in someone's life.

Mama and Daddy

My Dad was a tough man's man all the way but was also loving and gentle. He knew how to comfort us sons with his steady watch care over us. He was usually in an easy-going mood, unless I got the family car stuck in the mud on some backroad coming home from the nearest place a teenager in my hometown could buy beer!

Mama, on the other hand, was generally in a confrontational mood. She challenged my youthful efforts at manhood on a daily basis! She called me to impossible heights. Sallie Buckley probably influenced my life for good more than any other person. But it wasn't a lot of fun!

Don't condemn the hard voices in your life. Jesus said a lot of hard things. Can you imagine one of His followers saying, "Lord, that doesn't sound like you. That doesn't sound like love." Wait! He is love! The next time you get a hard word from someone remember, it might have to do with both the person's spiritual temperament and their assignment from God. Try to be open and listen.

There is a difference in a hard word and a harsh one. We as followers of Jesus are never called to be mean. Jesus comforted people but His goal was never to make them comfortable. It was Him who said, "Let the dead bury the dead. You follow me." (Matt.8:22) Thank you, Daddy, for showing me what tough and tender look like in a man. Thank you, Mama, for challenging me to never be satisfied with anything but my best. I love and miss you both so much!

Yesterday's Pain

I broke three bones at different times while playing football. Doctors were able to put them back together and I continued to play with no problems. But now, decades later, those same bones bring me much pain. They are an example of the truth about our old relationship wounds. When you got hurt, abused, or abandoned years ago you may have experienced a measure of healing but sometimes the pain waits. Wounds of the heart and soul can last a lifetime if we don't possess a rugged intentionality for dealing with them. From my own experience, here are some things we need for getting healed from old wounds to the heart and soul:

1. Brute-force honesty. The hardest time for me to be honest is when it's about me. I cannot do this without the help of the One Who created me. We all have different levels of relationship brokenness. Ask God if your hurt is hurting your current relationships not to mention your own well-being.

2. Healing relationships. We were born for intimacy with God and others. When those who should have loved us hurt us, it throws off our center of gravity. Getting healed from the inside out will take life-giving relationships with willing, loving people, and the one who promised "for better or for worse". Learning to trust people may be the biggest battle of your life.

3. Tenacious forgiveness. Forgiveness is not a one-time event. It is an enduring motivation that must

be stewarded every day. Forgiving someone may be a lifetime commitment!

4. Transformational objective. A plan from God gives the pains of life a purpose. Ask God every day what your life should look like in Him. There's no small or big service to God. Even the smallest act of kindness can become a miracle in someone's life.

Good Fathers

My Dad was a great man! He left me in the big woods to hunt by myself when I was barely in school. I was scared out of my skin, but he matter-of-factly told me I would not die! On our farm he gave me major responsibilities before I had the maturity to steward them. He completely turned me over to my coaches expecting me to navigate my relationships with them. He gave me independence in the world of men!

Daddy always pointed me toward the frontier of my life, expecting me to learn to win battles against adversity. Life with Rupert Buckley was not comfortable. Yet, every single night until I went to college he would come sit on the edge of my bed. He would ask me how I was, then the two of us would pray together. Every night for 18 years. He comforted me in all my struggles, failures, and problems but he didn't rescue me from them. Daddy left room for faith and growth for which I am eternally grateful!

As followers of Jesus, it's important to note the difference in being comfortable and being comforted. Comfortable people can afford to be kind. But the Lord does His transformational work in us when we are uncomfortable! But like my Dad, He never abandons us but comes close beside us every day. Even though I walk through the valley of the shadow of death, I will not fear for He will stand beside me, a good Father. (Psalm 23:4)

What did you bring into camp?

August is a time of discovery for football players. It's a make-or-break reality that determines the course of your season, and often the course of your life. The blood and sweat have a way of finding the weakness in you. Half-hearted attitudes and selfish motivations are driven out of your system like a stomach bug on its last fling. Every time you hang up your pads after practice, it's one more opportunity stay or go, to hold on to some comfort you have fallen in love with.

And when your head hit that pillow at night, your heart demanded an answer—"What did you bring into camp! What negative attitude is in you that will hurt all of us? What sense of entitlement or personal ambition do you carry that will get us beat in the 4th quarter of our rival game?"

There was a time when God put a ban on certain things that, if brought into the camp of the Israelites, would kill faith and unleash compromise among His people. But the ban was broken with the result that Israel was soundly defeated by its enemy. (See Joshua 6 and 7) They were in love with their way and got blinded to God's heart.

As followers of Jesus, the only thing that can prevent us from experiencing God's grace and freedom is stuff under the ban—unforgiveness, self-pity, blame-shifting, pouting, pride, and entitlement. Don't wait til the 4th quarter of your life to deal with that stuff. Do it now so we can get the true gift of who you are! And whatever you do, don't bring it into the camp of your family, your church, or your team.

When Empty Is Full

The astronauts of the Apollo 11 mission were the first people to land on the moon. These courageous men spent 22 hours collecting data and moon rocks. The extra weight of the rocks meant that they had to land the lunar module with only 21 seconds of fuel left. Too much fuel plus the moon rocks meant the craft would be too heavy to take off from the moon's surface. A gallon of fuel was the difference in success and failure of an epic accomplishment!

You and I were born for epic accomplishments—divine purpose and pursuit that demands we live lean and free of excess baggage. Here are some people I know who had to get lean to follow Jesus:

1. Mary Buckley who stood alone with God for years in our broken marriage.

2. Mississippi FCA's Hillary Ford who walked away from the drug life to follow Jesus.

3. Johnny and Debbie Buckner who left American affluence to serve God in Asia.

4. Coach Jeff Terrill who gave up a successful coaching career for full-time ministry.

5. Mike Cavanaugh who got all-in to pioneer singles' ministry in the US.

To accomplish great things, each of these people had to lean down and get rid of the excess baggage of an average life. What does excess baggage look like for you? Ask God about it. Read what Jesus says about it in Luke 18:18-30. Sometimes there's only a gallon of something between your success and failure! My goal in life? To die with an empty tank!

Halloween Truth

I believed in the devil before I believed in God. I knew him well, but without the light of Jesus I didn't understand his game. Satan is not a skinny little red man with a pitchfork we recognize at Halloween. He is the antichrist, one of the great powers on earth who controls whole nations and people groups. The Bible defines him as having extraordinary authority and cosmic power, a dynamic spiritual force of darkness across the earth and the spirit world. (Ephesians 6:11-12)

I highlight this not so that you will be afraid but so that you will be alert! As we live our lives led by the Holy Spirit, we will gain victory over Satan, but we must understand his tactics. "Often, we presume our spiritual enemies to be weak until they're not!" (Pastor Matt Murphy)

It doesn't help to beat our chests and yell at Satan like gladiators. We are told to run for the Lord's cover by being obedient to His word and His purpose for us. "The name of the LORD is a strong tower, the righteous run into it, and are safe." (Proverbs 18:10) We don't run from fear, we run from faith! Satan is powerful, we are weak, but God is light-years more powerful! It's not a lack of courage to run to God in times of trouble, it's the only smart move in the face of very real darkness.

Finish

Trey Hobson was a blocking back from Pascagoula, MS who you've never heard of. I will always remember him for what he said and did in MS Gulf Coast Community College's game in 2007 against Jones CC. Late in the fourth quarter, Gulf Coast was clinging to a 20-16 lead and had the ball on their own 34-yard line. Gulf Coast head coach Steve Campbell had his offense huddled up on the sideline challenging them to hold on to the ball and win the game. That's when Trey Hobson stepped inside that huddle and said, "Run it behind me. We ain't losin'!"

Coach Campbell took him at his word! Gulf Coast drove the ball straight at Jones' for the win with Trey blocking like a wild man. Three weeks later Gulf Coast played in and won the JUCO National Championship! Trey Hopson didn't score a TD or get his name in the paper. He faithfully opened holes for his teammates who got all the glory. This amazing athlete is the definition of a finisher, someone who faithfully and unselfishly works for the success of others.

Man, do we ever need finishers today! What if every dad told his children, "Come on kids, run it behind me. I'm never leaving and we ain't losin'." What if every husband told his wife, "Run it behind me, Girl! You can count on me to be here! We ain't losin'". Finishers are the game-changers the world desperately needs. It doesn't matter how you started. It matters how you finish.

"For which one of you when he wants to build a tower does not sit down and calculate the cost to see if he has enough to complete it? Otherwise, when he has laid a foundation, and is not able to finish, all who observe it begin to ridicule him saying, 'This man began to build and was not able to finish.'"—Luke 14:28-30)

Marriage Blood

In ancient Israel, a marriage and a wedding were two different things. The families of the bride and groom (including the children!) came together in an open field. A tent was set up in the middle of the congregation. As the families gathered around, the bride and groom entered the tent and had sex. The groom would then throw the sheet with the bride's blood on it over the wall of the tent. The people rejoiced and the wedding celebration began! The marriage was consummated in the act of sexual union. Then the wedding took place—the celebration of the blood on the sheet signifying the blood of the sacrifice. This is so powerful!

In God's design, when a man and woman have sexual intercourse, they become one, whether there was a wedding or not. In His eyes they are married. Sexual union initiates the covenant with the blood of the bride. Think about that for a minute. The act of sex completely uncovers the woman. If the man does not take her as his bride, she remains spiritually and emotionally unguarded and unprotected.

Read the stories of Amnon and Tamar (2 Samuel 13) and also Ruth and Naomi (the book of Ruth). Men, if you had sex with her, in God's eyes you married her! No wonder our culture is so broken! We have left millions of our women married without a wedding, without any provision! Men, it's our responsibility to protect our women from carrying the weight of a marriage covenant without us! If we don't, Christ-centered marriages will die and so will our culture.

PEACE

"Be anxious for nothing, but in everything by prayer and supplication with thanksgiving let your requests be made known to God. And the peace of God, which surpasses all comprehension, will guard your hearts and your minds in Christ Jesus." (Phil. 4:6-7)

Gulf of Mexico Gulfport, Mississippi

Left-Lane Crazy

There's more peace in the right lane. There came a time when I started driving the actual posted speed limit. If the sign said 55, I drove 55. If it said 65, I drove 65, all in the right lane of course. You only save a few minutes in the long run when you are driving 10 to 15 mph above the speed limit, which the vast majority of us do, right? There's so much tension, anger, and competition in that left lane, the so-called passing lane. But if you stay in the right lane and drive the posted speed limit, you will be surprised at the peace and rest you can experience, even on that short commute to work.

Posted speed limits make me want to ask you, what is the current speed of your life? I spoke with a guy the other day who has 3 kids. His wife works and all those kids are involved in community sports leagues. Their lives are in the 80 mph range—lots of tension, frustration, and competition with the Joneses. Like many of us, this guy stays in the left lane and is quickly driving toward a family wreck.

Is your current lifestyle worth the left lane? What will it take for you to drive sensibly? Don't make the mistake of thinking, "Well this is only a season of our lives. We'll slow down when the kids get older." But by the time they are in college, it's often too late. Your marriage, your body, and your mind will have been so abused by the fast lane of life that you can no longer find your heart or be yourself.

Here's a description of what it's like following Jesus Christ on His highway—"A highway will be there, a roadway, and it will be called the Highway of Holiness. The unrepentant will not travel on it,...and fools will not wander on it. No lion will be there, nor will any vicious beast go up on it. These will not be found there. But those who have been born again in Christ will walk there, and they will be glad. (Isaiah 35:8-10) Our whole lives depend on finding God's right lane!

Pacesetter

Mom and Dad, are you going at the speed of your family? The 20th century was a time of unmatched change in our nation as we moved from an agricultural economy to an industrial economy. The pace of rural life gave way to the hectic pace of company mandates, quotas, and deadlines. We were able to buy more, go more, and want more. We moved from a contemplative people to a multi-tasking people.

Remember that old church song about the Lord, "He's got the whole world in His hands"? Well, now you and I got the whole world in our hands! It's called a mobile phone! The problem is not the technology. The real threat is allowing the technology to get the best of your life, it's the possibility of losing our souls and our families in the crush of culture.

But this is not a new problem. Centuries ago, a man named Jacob got a job change and was moving his family. He wisely saw the weight of his decision on his family. His response was brave and clear—"My children are small and weak as are my cattle and sheep. If they are driven hard, they will not survive. Please allow me to travel at their pace." (Genesis 33:13-14)

Moms and Dads, are you going at the speed of your family? What is a healthy pace you them and you? Let's pray for one another, pray for clarity about how our work habits and schedules are impacting our families and our own souls. May God give you the grace to live your life at His pace for you and your family. Ask Him about it. He has a plan. I don't want you to have to deal with the regrets I carry because I couldn't say no to the expectations of others at the expense of my wife and children.

The Highway of Peace

When I was learning to drive with my Dad as my teacher, we watched as another driver sped around us and several other cars at excessive speeds. Several miles down the road was a small town with a few stop lights. As we pulled up to the last light, Dad pointed out the car next to us waiting for the light to change. It was the speeding, tailgating driver that just passed all of us.

Dad's lesson was that, in his impatience, that driver had put all of us in danger but gained nothing. What a great lesson about the power of patience! Patience is not simply the ability to wait, it's how we act while we're waiting! Patience is the outward sign of inner faith and peace.

Here's what the Lord tells us about patience—

1. "Be still before the Lord and wait patiently for him; do not fret when people succeed in their ways when they carry out their wicked schemes." (Psalm 37:7)

2. "The Lord will fight for you; you need only to be still." (Exodus 14:14)

3. "Let us not become weary in doing good, for at the proper time we will reap a harvest if we do not give up." (Galatians 6:9)

4. "Better a patient person than a warrior, one with self-control than one who takes a city." (Pro. 16:32)

Stopwatch Vacations

I remember taking family vacations when our kids were small. Sadly, I also remember trying to get everywhere in record time and hurrying everybody out of McDonalds so we could "stay on schedule". Looking back, I can see that I was often driving my family instead of leading them. Pushing the envelope on vacations was nothing more than a reflection of my entire life at the time. I was like that homeless guy in our town. Whenever you see him, it looks like he is hustling down the street to get to some appointment. There is no appointment. He is going fast to nowhere.

Is that you? Remember what Jacob told Esau out on the edge of the wilderness? Esau and his army were accompanying Jacob and his family as they were traveling toward Esau's home. Think about that for a minute—an army of trained men leading a family with kids. Jacob saw the danger and told Esau, "Please pass on before me your servant, and I will travel according to the pace of my family." (Genesis 33:12-14) Now that's rich wisdom! Dad and Mom, whether you are on vacation or not, don't let your "army" lead your family. Praying for you to find the inner peace of the Lord so you can find the right pace for your loved ones.

"Love is patient and kind; love does not envy or boast; it is not arrogant or rude. It does not insist on its own way; it is not irritable or resentful; it does not rejoice at wrongdoing but rejoices with the truth. Love bears all things, believes all things, hopes all things, endures all things. Love never ends". 1 Corinthians 13:4-8

POVERTY AND WEALTH

"The rich and the poor have this in common: The LORD is the Maker of them all." (Proverb 22:2)

Cat Island, Mississippi Sound

A Place at the Table

Recently I witnessed two homeless people fighting over a homeless street corner. They were arguing about which one would get to beg from that spot for the day. The whole time this was happening, our good Father was right there with them! You know, the One who owns it all—the cattle on a thousand hills, all the wealth of earth, and that street corner. They just couldn't see.

This is a living illustration of poverty and wealth, that there is only one decision between those two realities. Jesus addressed this street corner when He said, "To you it has been granted to know the mysteries of the kingdom of heaven, but to them it has not been granted. For whoever has, to him more shall be given, and he will have an abundance; but whoever does not have, even what he has shall be taken away from him." (Matthew 13:10-12)

This is not a statement about predestination, it's a teaching on the very real effect of spiritual starvation. "What is the source of quarrels and conflicts among you? Is not the source your pleasures that wage war in your members? You lust and do not have; so you commit murder. You are envious and cannot obtain; so you fight and quarrel. You do not have because you do not ask. You ask and do not receive, because you ask with wrong motives, so that you may spend it on your pleasures." (James 4:1-8)

Translation—When you believe your cup is always half empty, you lose the capacity to see the Lord's provision and the needs of others. When you see that the cup of the Lord is always running over, you become confident in His provision, whatever it may be. Are you fighting for some trashy street corner when God is offering you His kingdom!

"Draw near to God and He will draw near to you" is both a command and a promise. "Cleanse your hands, you sinners; and purify your hearts, you double-minded"—this is not a word of condemnation but of loving reproach. The unrepentant person—one who can't see his life from a kingdom of God viewpoint, will always be the beggar. The difference in being spiritually bankrupt and being spiritually hungry is the difference in a homeless beggar and a beloved child. We don't have to fight for a place at our Father's table!

Show Me the Money

American Howard Hughes was one of the richest men in the world with a net worth of 11 billion dollars! Yet, he lived the last years of his life in squalor, terrified of germs and of physical contact with other people. He died alone in an apartment full of nothing, all his billions in a Swiss bank account!

This amazingly gifted individual illustrates a powerful truth—poverty is not about your net worth, it's about your self-worth. It's an internal reality fueled by the values you carry in your heart. Howard Hughes died from poverty though he was filthy rich! Money will never defeat poverty, only changed hearts. Look at the 4 cultures below. Where did you come from? Where do you live now? How can you bring your culture of origin under the culture of God's Kingdom?

Poverty culture rules and values:

1. Money/material possessions: chaotic—to be spent
2. Time: the present. Decisions are made for the moment based on feelings and survival.
3. Destiny: believe in fate, cannot change the present or the future.
4. Worldview: see the world in terms of local neighborhood or hometown—my people.
5. Driving forces: survival, spending.

Middle class culture rules and values:

1. Money/material possessions: to be managed.
2. Time: future most important. Decisions made for future investments.
3. Destiny: believes in choice. Can change the future with good choices today.
4. Worldview: see the world in terms of national setting.

5. Driving forces: work, achievement.

Wealthy culture rules and values:

1. Money/material possessions: to be saved and invested.

2. Time: traditions/legacy most important. Decisions made to build legacy.

3. Destiny: obligation to be honorable, generous, and responsible.

4. Worldview: see the world in terms of international setting.

5. Driving forces: relationships—social, political, and financial connections.

Kingdom of God Culture values:

1. Money/material possessions: limitless under God's guidance.

2. Time: Past, present, and future all connected to God's plan and purpose.

3. Destiny: sons and daughters of a King Who owns it all.

4. Worldview: see the world from heaven's perspective.

5. Driving forces: God's loving plan and purpose.

You may not get to choose to move from a poverty culture to a wealth culture, but everyone who surrenders their lives to Christ gets to live in the Kingdom of God Culture. That doesn't mean instant wealth, it means forever care, provision, and love! "My God shall supply all your needs

according to His riches and glory in Christ Jesus!"
(Philippians 4:19))

Million-Dolla Boys

In the South poverty, religion, and football are brothers of
necessity. These three realities draw from one another and
feed a starving culture born of desperation and lack. It's
not a Black problem or a white problem. It's not a rich
problem or a poor problem. It's a followers-of-Jesus
problem.

From tenant houses to our fabulously wealthy college
football stadiums, our lives are woven into one story.
"What's 4th and 1 yard to a player who knows how to miss
a meal?" (Jason Sparks, college football coach.) "If I leave
here, where am I gonna go?" (Jimmy Rowster, struggling
with the idea of Life After Football)

In a poverty culture, children are our currency and baby
mamas our banks. A 20-year-old fatherless kid can earn a
university millions of dollars and wind up on the streets in
less than a year! Damn. Between music that would shame
hell and sex with a future single mother, we recite the
Lord's prayer with the fervency of evangelists. It's not just
hypocrisy. It's devastation.

What can we do? What should you do? All of us who are aware of these facts are accountable. We can all pray. We can all stop ignoring the ugly underbelly of athletic wealth. If you buy a game ticket, you accountable. We can all identify a former player who needs guidance, resources, and prayer.

Don't say ignorant things like, "Well, we paid for his college education." If you figure that by an eight-hour day, that kid was making about a dollar an hour! We can be a catalyst for change. I don't yet know what that looks like for all of us, but I know what it looks like for me! Together let's ask the Lord for His solutions. At your school, you are all family whether you want to be or not!

Too Tight

Paddling a kayak with a double-bladed paddle is much easier than it looks, but you would never know it when you see a beginner trying to do it. Most of the rookies I have trained over-paddle by grabbing the paddle tightly and putting all their strength into every stroke. When they see they are getting nowhere slowly, they double up their efforts resulting in weariness and frustration. The secret to efficient paddling is to hold the paddle lightly instead of gripping it tightly. This allows the paddle blades to hit the water at the perfect angle and an easy pull is all you need to get moving.

God's blessings are like kayak paddles. We've got to hold them lightly. If you grab them and try to force them to do your will, you will never know the power and benefit in them that God intended.

My wife, my children, and my health are all blessings from God but if my attitude toward them is anxiety, fear, and possessiveness I only wear myself out, unable to enjoy what only God could give. If you are prospering financially, enjoy the season of increase. Give big, don't hoard your wealth as it can be gone in a minute. Blessings are beautiful but you can choke the life out of them by demanding that they serve you. Hold them lightly, even your children, and rejoice in the Lord, thanking Him for all good things! "And God is able to make all grace abound to you, so that having all sufficiency in all things at all times, you may abound in every good work." (2 Cor. 9:8)

Free To Work

Equality is where our government gives everybody the same opportunity resulting in the growth of initiative and potential. Equity is where our government gives everybody the same outcome benefit resulting in the growth of apathy and entitlement. The one creates increase while the other creates dependency.

This equation is so much like the Gospel. God gives all of us opportunity to reach our full potential through His purpose for us. His provision for each of us is different and given according to his wisdom. Our natural talent, IQ, and temperament all come from Him for a specific purpose.

If in a free country I demand to be compensated on the level of someone with an extraordinary business mind, which I do not possess, both he and I will eventually suffer loss. His will be financial loss, mine will be loss of dignity and purpose. Let's pray for our country in these days. Much is to be won and lost through the concepts of equality and equity. By all means let's liberally help the poor and needy but by our own choice and not government laws. Here are some important truths from God on the subject:

1. "Whatever you do, do it with all your heart, as for the Lord and not for men." (Colossians 3:23)

2. "The soul of the lazy craves and gets nothing, while the soul of the diligent is richly supplied." (Proverbs 13:4)

3. "Commit your work to the Lord, and your plans will be established. (Proverbs 16:3)

4. "Aspire to live quietly, and to mind your own affairs, and to work with your hands, as we instructed you, so that you may walk properly

before outsiders and be dependent on no one." (1 Thess. 4:11)

5. "In all things I have shown you that by working hard in this way we must help the weak and remember the words of the Lord Jesus, how he himself said, 'It is more blessed to give than to receive.'" (Acts 20:35)

More or Less?

Poverty is a cruel taskmaster. It saddens me to see it in its many forms in my home state of Mississippi. We have failed to realize that money and education will never fix the problem. Being in poverty doesn't mean you don't have anything. It means you have a wrong attitude about whatever you do have. Here are some sure signs of a poverty mentality:

- You give the Lord what's left instead of what's first. (Malachi 3:10)

- You don't understand the difference between accumulating and increasing. (Luke 16:10)

- You ignore the poor. (Ecclesiastes 5:10-12)

- You constantly worry about your finances because you trust more in what your money can do for you than what God can do for you. (1 Tim. 6:17-19)

- You identify as a sinner instead of as a son/daughter. (Luke 15)

- You miss God's provision because you have a narrow definition of wealth. (Matt. 16:26)

- You don't believe that the Lord is fundamentally generous. (Jeremiah 29:11)

God intends for the church to steward the wealth of nations for the health of all people! (Isaiah 60) It all starts with you. When you get offended at pastors and churches for asking for money, you are only revealing your own fear and insecurity, a sure sign of poverty. Today, let's approach the Lord with open hearts and open hands. If you don't want to give to a church, stop going there! Start walking out into your community. Find poverty and wisely give to it.

RELIGION

"For this is the love of God, that we keep His commandments; and His commandments are not burdensome. For whatever is born of God overcomes the world; and this is the victory that has overcome the world—our faith." (I John 5:3-4)

Pearl River Marsh (See gator!)

No Payments Ever

Mississippi State University paid my whole college bill for 4 years. One of my close friends got no scholarship and finally paid off his college debt after 20 years! We both owed what we could not pay. My friend struggled for years coming up with what he owed every month. I signed a paper before I even entered college and it was a done deal. No payments ever.

Most of us work our whole lives trying to pay the debt for our mistakes, our failures, and our wrongs. We do good deeds, give to the poor at Christmas time, and try to get to church if we can. All the while Jesus has a full scholarship with your name on it. All He asks is for a commitment, just like a coach asks for a player's commitment. Sign up from the heart and experience new life forever! Jesus paid your whole bill at the Cross! No payments ever! Thank you, Lord!

Matthew 7:11
If you then, being evil, know how to give good gifts to your children, how much more will your Father who is in heaven give what is good to those who ask Him!

Romans 6:23
For the wages of sin is death, but the free gift of God is eternal life in Christ Jesus our Lord.

1 Corinthians 14:1
Pursue love, yet desire earnestly spiritual *gifts,* but especially that you may prophesy.

Ephesians 2:8
For by grace you have been saved through faith; and that not of yourselves, *it is* the gift of God;

James 1:17
Every good thing given and every perfect gift is from above, coming down from the Father of lights, with whom there is no variation or shifting shadow.

Turn Up the Light

I'm amazed at some of the tools my kids are using to raise their kids. For instance, the use of healthy practices for establishing emotional connection between them and their children. What they are doing is a long way from "Shut up or I'll give you something to cry about!" Their children are healthier because their parents are more knowledgeable than we were.

Though not all changes in parent-child relationship are good, child-rearing "truth" looks different today and I'm glad. Those truths were available to parents back in the day, but moms and dads of yesteryear were only operating out of what they had been taught themselves. Greater knowledge was available, but they had no context for it and no experience to validate it.

This is a prime example of the history of biblical truth and how we can fight dead religion with honor. When I think back on some things I was taught as a young Christian by older, more knowledgeable leaders, I can see that some concepts that appeared profound at the moment now seem elementary. But instead of judging those leaders as less worthy, we should remember that they were moving in the truth they had in that season. That's all God ever asks right? We should remain grateful for their teachings and instruction, the foundation for greater understanding of truth.

Truth doesn't increase. Revelation of the truth increases! The dawn of knowledge is new every morning! (2 Samuel 23:4) Jesus is the same yesterday, today, and forever but our understanding of Him is not! (Hebrews 13:8) The revelation of Christ is like the rising of the sun. The light just keeps getting brighter and brighter! (Psalm 113) Greater truth is increasingly available to the Christian and the church. If we are connected to the Source, we will have context for it and experience to validate it! Our children will be healthier spiritually because they have more Light!

Are You Religious?

They don't know what they are saying when they call Christianity a religion. Maybe in your culture it is a religion rather than what it was meant to be—life born from wholehearted faith in the one true God, the God of

Abraham, Isaac, and Jacob, the Father of Jesus Christ—
that God.

The Creator did not establish a religion with Adam and
Eve. He established His presence with them based on a
Father's promise of love for His children. But Adam and
Eve chose to do something instead of be something—the
very definition of religion. When God raised up a people
called Israel, He asked them to pursue Him and stay close
to Him like children do a good father. But they wanted a
set of rules instead of His beautiful presence. So, God gave
them a book of laws called the Old Testament.

Then God did the unthinkable. He sent His own Son as a
living testimony of everything that went before—every law,
every ritual, every tradition—revealed as the image and
Person of God Himself. It was a New Promise that soon
became known as the New Testament. But God's people
came to worship the Bible instead of Him.

Somehow in our humanness we prefer words on a page
rather than the One we cannot see. Maybe because it's
safer and more familiar, a belief system that allows us to
call ourselves "sorry sinners" so that we can be more
comfortable in our sin instead of being convicted by God's
living Presence.

Coming near to a God who is alive is not for the
fainthearted. He is so good, but He is so not safe. But the

greater danger is trying to keep rules, enforce doctrines, and worship rituals. The written word itself testifies against religion calling it devotion to these things instead of to God. (Acts 26:5) Religion is fueled by zeal rather than love for God. ("For I can testify about them that they are zealous for God, but their zeal is not based on knowledge (In Hebrew this word knowledge is "yada" meaning "intimacy."—Romans 10:2.)

Religion is so deadly that 90% of the New Testament is an attack against it! How do we fight religion? There are two equally dangerous positions for the follower of Christ. The first is to be led into valuing your denominational traditions and doctrines more than you value the Person and Presence of the living, abiding Christ. The second approach is, in an attempt to be free from religion, we reject urgent written truths that describe the heart, mind, and purposes of God—commands and principles that guide us to Him.

This is the reason He sent us the Holy Spirit, a Person, not a prayer book. Without His daily guidance we are lost from God's Presence. Ask Him to reveal Himself to you. Ask Him to show you any anger, offense, rebellion, or laziness in you that is blinding your eyes to Him. Ask Him to help you to hear His voice. Go sit with Him! "Therefore the Lord longs to be gracious to you, and therefore He waits on high to have compassion on you. For the Lord is a God of

291

justice, how blessed are all those who long for Him."
(Isaiah 30:18) One of the most stunning truths of all time—
God waits for you!

Street Corner Faith

I know a guy who was born into a messed up, dysfunctional family. He basically raised himself and seemed destined to the same desperate poverty. Still just a teenager, he attended a revival meeting with thousands of other people and gave his life to the Jesus Christ. He had no Christian or church experience whatsoever. All He had was a desperate, hungry heart and the Holy Spirit.

One of the first things he ever did as a new Christian was to stand on the street corner of his city every Saturday morning. He told everyone who came by him about Jesus Christ and his new life. A tall, skinny teenager on a street corner in New York. It's what he could do.

If you follow the Lord, sooner or later you are not going to look normal.

Allowing people to take advantage of you for some purpose of God might look foolish to others. Giving to someone who is not responsible enough to wisely steward your gift makes you look gullible. The Pharisees really thought that Jesus was weak because he could not even save Himself.

So, who will you look like today? Pause this morning and ask God to move your heart for those who are lost and hurting. Be willing to step out of your comfort zone and do something for them.

Oh, by the way, that skinny kid sharing his faith on the street corner? His name is Mike Cavanaugh and in the last 30 years God has used him in remarkable ways as a nationally recognized evangelist, Bible school president, and leader of leaders. Small start. Big influence. Faithfulness is not giving something big. It's giving what you have. "As each one has received a special gift, employ it in serving one another as good stewards of the manifold grace of God." (I Peter 4:10)

Wearing The Colors

When I was in high school, I admired Auburn University football that featured 2 All-Americans—QB Pat Sullivan and WR Terry Beasley. I wore Auburn jerseys and hung Auburn symbols in my bedroom. I never attended a game, gave money to athletics, or sacrificed for the Auburn program in any way. I just admired the War Eagle symbol. I just wore the colors.

There was a time when I did the same thing with Christianity. I wore the Cross but it was never more than a trinket for me. The Cross is the most widely recognized Christian symbol in the world, adorning millions of churches and chapels. We wear it as jewelry and position it in public places. We put in on our stationary and erect it along our highways.

In the middle of all the public display, has the Cross lost its meaning and purpose for you? May we not forget, we don't worship the cross. We use it to draw us back to the One we do worship. Meanings of the cross:

- It means an instrument of torture and death.
- It means blood.
- It means reckoning and reconciliation.
- It means fulfilled prophecies.
- It means surrender and love.
- It means purpose and passion.
- It means forgiveness and life.
- It means an end and a beginning.
- It means eternity.

The Cross. It's not just rugged. It's eternal! May we not display it lightly.

Pure Salvation

Getting saved is not a formula or a to-do list. We don't attain salvation through any act on our part whatsoever. Salvation is the purest experience on the planet, which is why Satan tries to contaminate it with all manner of religious works and formulas.

Many people use Romans 10:8 as a rule of thumb about how to "get saved". It says, "that if you confess with your mouth Jesus as Lord and believe in your heart that God raised Him from the dead, you will be saved." But the word "confess" in this verse does not mean to declare or acknowledge one's sins. It's the Greek word "homolego" and it means "to say the same thing as or to agree with".

In other words, if you are truly born again, you will see sin like Jesus does and respond like He would. The idea is that a person's mouth communicates the true conviction and attitude of his heart, agreeing with Christ's word and His heart in all matters.

Confession is not just telling God about your sins. It's fully agreeing with Him in the whole of your life! The purity of salvation is experienced only through the unadulterated surrender of one's heart. It's not about doing anything. It's about quitting everything and giving up, giving up completely to what Jesus Christ already did. Salvation is His work, not yours in any form or fashion. If you attach one ounce of your sweat to that moment, it ceases to be a work of pure grace and becomes, at least in part, what you did.

I fear that there are millions of people who think they are saved because they said a prayer and "confessed" their sins. Confession of sin is an important thing to do to stay in right relationship with God (I John 1:8-9) but it never results in salvation. Only a surrendered heart does. "For by grace you have been saved through faith. And this is not your own doing; it is the gift of God, not a result of works, so that no one may boast." (Ephesians 2:8-9)

Are you really saved? Are you really surrendered? If you have any doubts whatsoever take these things to the Lord. He is so willing to show you the Way. "In Him, you also, after listening to the message of truth, the gospel of your salvation—having also believed, you were sealed in Him with the Holy Spirit of promise, who is given as a pledge of our inheritance, with a view to the redemption of God's own possession, to the praise of His glory." (Eph. 1:13-14) It's all about Him!

I Know Him

Several years ago, I read famous football coach Tony Dungy's book called "Uncommon". I really enjoyed reading about his highly successful career as a football coach and his bold faith in Christ. Several years later the Fellowship of Christian Athletes invited Coach Dungy to be the keynote speaker at a fundraising event in Mississippi. It was my job to attend to his needs the short time he was with us. This allowed me the privilege of about an hour of conversation with this renowned player and coach.

I was amazed at how much I learned about Coach Dungy that I didn't get from his book by hearing his voice, observing his attitude toward me, and watching how he treated autograph seekers and doormen. As I got to know the author, the book took on new meaning!

There's another book I read having never met the author. It's called the Bible. For years the only thing I knew about Jesus was some words on a page. But then one day I heard His voice calling me. He took me up on the mountain of His presence and showed me His heart! I got to know the Author and the book took on new meaning!

Jesus says it's entirely possible to read the Bible and not know Him. "You search the Scriptures because you think that in them you have eternal life; it is these that testify about Me." (John 5:39) My heart had to stand next to His heart to hear His testimony, then His book came to life!

What about you? What kind of response do you have to the Bible? Did you read parts of it and not understand it or feel like you gained anything from it? Have the words of the Bible ever been an urgent part of your life? Good News! Jesus wants to be known! Keep pursuing Him!

1. "I love those who love Me, and those who diligently seek Me will find Me." (God in Proverb 8:17)

2. "Seek the Lord and His strength, seek His face continually." (I Chronicles 16:11)

3. "Evil men do not understand justice. But those who seek the Lord understand all things." (Proverb 28:5)

Extravagant

I belonged to a local church one time where this middle-aged man would show up alone every Sunday. He never spoke to anybody, nor did he get involved in any way. He just showed up, sat through the services, and walked out. What would you call a man like that? A bit strange, uncommitted, lukewarm? Maybe he had a social disorder or just didn't like other people.

There's another possibility worth considering. What if he was giving the highest and the best he could possibly give? What if he was the male side of the parable of the widow's mite? Remember her? One morning at church, she put a single penny into the offering plate. Jesus was there watching with His disciples.

As He always did, the Lord saw the woman's heart, not just her actions. He pointed out that she found a way to give though she had almost nothing. The Lord called it extravagant! That middle-aged man? Maybe just showing up at church was an extravagant gift from him. God is the only one worthy to measure what anybody gives or withholds.

Better Than Better

I watched an ugly high school football game this past season. Neither team looked disciplined or focused. In a postgame interview, one of the coaches surprised everybody with his summary of the game. He said it was the best game his team had played all year! He told reporters he had some young guys who had rarely ever won, that most of them came from tough backgrounds with lots of unhealthy distractions. He was thrilled with their performance because he knew the whole story and could see great potential that others couldn't.

That team reminds me of me as I was becoming a walk-on for God's team. In my first year as a Christian, I drank 3 or 4 beers most days. You might've been tempted to say, "He either has no character or is not even a Christian." Actually, I had a lot of character because I had completely stopped using all the illegal drugs that had been a part of my life for years. And I was most assuredly a Christian because I had genuinely given my life to Jesus. I no longer attended crazy parties and started learning how to be faithful to my wife.

Considering where I had been, I was living a very disciplined life. But my discipline was related to my history with God, not my relationship with you. I've learned that when I am patient and interested enough to get the whole story about people, I can begin to see great promise and potential in them instead of only their current messes. As we help people, let's start with the wisdom of God and not the three beers! "Do not judge according to appearance, but judge with righteous judgment." (John 7:24)

Speak Up

Don't be afraid to question your faith. Some of the greatest Christian movements in history occurred because men and women questioned current church doctrine and tradition. The Great Reformation birthed Protestantism (a new faith movement) because ordinary people questioned church ideology of the time. High school and college kids of the 60's "Jesus Movement" not only questioned the traditions of the church, but the convictions of the church! Millions gave their lives to Christ! The Charismatic Movement became an unquenchable flame across the world because ordinary men and women discovered there was more to their faith than what they had been taught.

The fact that no human has ever discovered all "the riches of the glory of this mystery, which is Christ in you", is reason for all of us to keep seeking by questioning what we believe. Here are some important things to consider as we seek to know the fullness of the Gospel of Christ:

1. Complaining and whining are not helpful. We don't attack or devalue people or the church, we pursue Jesus and His truth in the Bible. (Romans 2)

2. Because we are called to love the Church, our response toward the Church and our church leaders should look like this: love, joy, peace, patience, kindness, goodness, faithfulness, gentleness, and self-control. (Galatians 5:22-23)

3. We should question ourselves before we question church doctrines and practices. Being humble with a teachable spirit is the doorway to truth. (I Peter 1:5)

4. We are called to honor our church leaders by treating them with great respect and forbearance. Communicate "faith questioning" directly to them. (Eph.4:2)

5. Our goal is the Presence and Purpose of Christ. Any other motive will distract us from His heart.

One of a Kind

Sallie Elizabeth Welch Buckley is my mother. What a woman! I've known few people in my life who had more personality, courage, and tenacity! Mama knew what she was about and wasn't too concerned with what you thought about it. She allowed no one to define her. A women's libber well before the Women's Lib Movement, she often frustrated convention and intimidated religion. Sounds like somebody else I know!

They didn't kill Jesus because he acted holier than everybody. They killed him because he would not allow anyone to define Him. He loved everybody but bowed to no one. When people went to Him with an agenda or some politically correct expectation, He would either openly confront them or just walk away. He hasn't changed you know. Jesus will not work for your political cause. He is not an American. He does not work for the gay people or the straight people, politically charged racial groups, or your favorite denomination.

He is a King of a Kingdom currently being established on the earth. He is the only one who has the authority and wisdom to define His work and you. In Him you can get a new storyline! The both of you get to finish the book! Don't let any influence other than the influence of His will write your life. Sallie Buckley lived as she died, true to God and true to herself. Thank you Mama for showing me the way!

Flea-bitten Faith

Years ago, I was driving on a country road and spotted a small furry animal right on the centerline. I was thinking "roadkill", but as I passed, I saw that it was a puppy very much alive! Thinking it might belong to someone I stopped to check it out.

That was the most flea-bitten, mangy dog I had ever seen! It had no collar and no sign of any ownership other than abuse. I took the dog home where Mary and I nursed it back to health. We named her Lucy, and she became my favorite dog ever. Sadly, she never got over her previous neglect and mistreatment. We never felt like we got the best of Lucy because of her fear and lack of trust in our love.

Many people are like my dog. They had a religious experience that was neglectful, unhealthy, or hurtful. In my conversations with non-Christians, I'm discovering that almost all of them have one thing in common—what they have rejected is not the One true God, but rather some distorted, religious, or immature form of Christianity.

There's only one thing worse than no knowledge of God and that's the wrong knowledge of God. It's a fact that the most productive evangelism occurs among completely unchurched people groups. Those raised in Christian catechisms, doctrines, and religious rituals often exhibit a hardening of the spiritual arteries. They become like Lucy, incredibly hard to reach.

If you want to pray an evangelistic prayer, pray for that growing number of people in America who are leaving the faith because they never had the faith. Jesus' words about them are true that "They are always seeing but never perceiving, hearing but not understanding, otherwise they would repent and be forgiven." (Mark 4:12) I used to be one of those hard-hearted people! Nobody is unreachable!

The "Good People" Rant

You cannot experience heaven if you haven't fallen in love with God. Conversion is not a prayer. It's when my heart becomes one with God's heart through love. Being saved is not a static spiritual exchange—your dirty laundry for God's holy nod. True repentance is not part of a salvation checklist. It's what a heart can't help but look like when it falls in love with the Lord.

He's waiting on love. That's why bad things still happen to so-called "good people". He's so patient that he wants no one to be lost, to be unloved. So, He waits. Don't blame your broken leg on Love. Stop jacking around with your religious traditions at the expense of compassion and justice. Get rid of all your pathetic defenses to His extraordinary ways of healing your life through His one-of-a-kind love.

Stop making the focus "the salvation prayer"! Teach people to hear God's voice! A person can be born again in a moment without a word. A heart turned toward God's heart will sooner or later find its voice, but it will be an authentic voice of conviction rather than ritual. That brand of confession will be the confession of love expressed by your changed attitudes and actions.

Finally, my confession is worthless without my heart! (Romans 10:9) "Beloved, let us love one another, for love is from God, and whoever loves has been born of God and knows God." (I John 1:7) "By this all people will know that you are my disciples, if you have love for one another." (John 13:35) "Anyone who does not love does not know God, because God is love." (I John 4:8) As followers of Christ, we don't define love by our feelings but by our actions and our attitudes.

Witnessing

Is your church stuck at the cross? Hebrews 6:1 addresses this problem—"Therefore leaving the elementary teaching about Christ, let us press on to maturity, not laying again a foundation of repentance from dead works and of faith toward God." The word "elementary" here means "beginning, origin; the person or thing that commences". This means the cross of Christ is always the starting place of faith but never the stopping place.

Remember Jesus' last meeting with His disciples chronicled in Acts? He went up into the clouds and, as His guys were standing their gawking, an angel said, "Why are you standing here looking into the sky? The Holy Spirit is about to fill you so you can go and conquer all pain and lostness!" (Acts 1:9-10 my paraphrase) At this point the Holy Spirit rolled out His gifts, His fruit, His power, and His supernatural love so we could be filled with the true nature of Christ to do what He did!

Are you still standing at the cross and gazing up at heaven, hoping Jesus will come back soon? If you are truly born again, He already came back in your born-again heart!! He clearly said, "Truly, truly, I say to you, he who believes in Me, the works that I do, he (my followers) will do also; and greater works than these he will do." (John 14:12)

The cross gave us the authority, the Holy Spirit gave us the power. Our love for Jesus is expressed as we complete the assignment that He gave us to "go into all the world and make disciples". I don't believe we've made a disciple until he or she is born again and filled with the Spirit doing what Jesus did!

Calling Out Gold

I had a coach who never gave any of us a personal compliment. No matter how we played, it was you shoulda' or you coulda'. His reasoning? "They will get 'the big head' and become lazy and self-centered." Maybe Christians are afraid to tell others about the great things in them because they are afraid of the same thing, that if we only encourage without evaluating, evangelizing, and correcting, they will take that as agreement with their current lifestyle.

Don't we have enough faith to give others our best encouragement and let the Holy Spirit do what only He can do? It's human nature to point out the negative but it's God's nature to point out awesomeness! "For since the creation of the world God's invisible qualities—his eternal power and divine nature—have been clearly seen, being understood FROM WHAT HAS BEEN MADE."—Romans 1:20 (my emphasis). That would be us!

How about we recognize "God's eternal power and divine nature" in everyone we meet! If people can get a revelation of Him in them or around them, it's usually enough for them to get a revelation of their sin—like when Peter saw Jesus fill his net with fish. "When Simon Peter saw this he fell at Jesus' knees and said, 'Go away from me, Lord; I am a sinful man!'" (Lk. 5:8).

"Let no unwholesome word proceed from your mouth, but only such a word as is good for edification according to the need of the moment, so that it will give grace to those who hear." (Ephesians 4:29)

You can change the whole direction of someone's life with only a few timely words!

SERVING

"For even the Son of Man did not come to be served, but to serve, and to give His life a ransom for many." (Mark 10:45)

Pelahatchie Bay Brandon, Mississippi

Role Player

In my first two years of playing football, I only got in the game if one of the starters needed to rest. I filled a spot on the kickoff and punt teams. In practice I ran the pass routes of our next opponent so our defensive backs could be prepared to stop them. Nobody watching those early games in my playing career would have predicted that I would become a starter for an SEC football team. I was a "role player", the most anonymous position on any team.

Being a role player is like basic training for would-be soldiers—no rewards, no accolades, and little encouragement. You show up, suit up, and give everything you have expecting nothing in return but blood and sweat. Role players are as vital to a team's success as the starting quarterback or the best linebacker. Without them nobody gets better. If an athlete never becomes a role player, he will not possess the humility and unselfishness that true greatness demands.

The phenomena of community league and travel ball teams is changing the face of American sport in a most disturbing way. We no longer expect our kids to become role players. Parents are the new athletic directors who control the power and the money. Their children no longer have to earn a spot on the field because Mom and Dad pay for that spot, expecting their kid to get immediate playing time.

Mom and Dad, you are the key to protecting your child from becoming a narcissistic athlete whose only interest is his own success. To live a healthy, productive life kids must learn to serve, to give, and to champion others. Let's stop promoting our kids and start training them to be role players who will become role models! I've never been the brightest or most talented person in the jobs I've had. But I did learn to be a role player. It has made the difference in my life, my devotion to God, and my future! Become brilliant in the basics! Be a role player!

"The greatest among you will be your servant." (Matthew 23:11)

Tough Like Larry Joe

One of the greatest football players I've ever known is a guy named Larry Joe Dykes. He was a fullback for our Starkville High School Football Team. During the 3 years he played we only lost 2 games and he was a big reason why. Larry Joe brought something that changes everything. He was tough. He wasn't the biggest or fastest player, but after every game he had blood on his face and turf sticking out of his helmet! Without even realizing it, my teammates and I rallied around him when adversity struck, because we knew he wasn't going to quit fighting. I'm a firm believer that "tough" trumps talent every time.

What's true in life is true in faith. I am privileged to know Christian missionaries to foreign nations. One thing they tell me is that when they come back home to America, they are astonished at how soft Americans are. We have the world's best recliners and mattresses, the best medical care and all the food we want. If you're an American, there's a strong chance that you are jaded—dulled by excess and hard to impress. Being jaded about material things is dangerous because it leads to being jaded about God.

Two of the most important people I know are Randall and Jean Ann Foxworth who spent years as missionaries in Papua New Guiana. They don't think like us who have 401k's and homes bigger than what we need. They've lived in jungles with almost no material possessions. Nevertheless, they are remarkably resilient and refreshing. They know they own "the cattle on a thousand hills" by faith in Jesus Christ. They are an example of why the Lord says, "Don't store up for yourselves treasures on earth, where moth and rust destroy, and where thieves break in and steal." (Matthew 6:19)

Ragtag Faith

When Wycliffe Bible translator Doug Meland and his wife moved into a village of Brazil's Fulnio Indians, he was referred to simply as "the white man." The term was by no means complimentary, since other white men had exploited these native Indians of their lands. But after the Melands learned the Fulnio language and began to help the people with medicine and many other things, they began calling Doug "the respectable white man." When the Melands began adopting the customs of the people, the Fulnio gave even greater acceptance and spoke of Doug as "the white Indian."

Then one day as Doug was washing the dirty, blood-caked foot of an injured Fulnio boy, he overheard the boy's mother say to another Indian: "Whoever heard of a white man washing an Indian's foot before? Certainly, this man is from God!" From that day on, whenever Doug would go into an Indian home, it was announced: "Here comes the man God sent us."

This true story reminds me of that day God bent down and washed the feet of His ragtag group of followers. It reminds me of the racial tension in our world. No law will ever overcome the bitterness and offense of racism. No government can mandate healing from poverty or racial privilege. It's going to take bent knees and dirty hands, helping others get rid of the dirt in their lives. It will take humility on a scale that many of us may not have experienced.

From "the white man" to "the man God sent us"—think about that transition as you spend this day. Ask God for His eyes so you can see what He sees. Ask him for the humility of heart to help someone in a way that makes you get down in their dirt. "God chose the lowly things of this world and the despised things—to nullify the things that are, so that no one may boast before Him." (I Cor. 1:28-29) People don't need our opinions, they need our hands and knees!

Taking The Heat

John Robert Fox was a soldier in the 92nd infantry division of the US Army in World War 2. On Christmas Day 1944, his division was forced to run from an Italian village as a much larger German battalion attacked them. Fox volunteered to stay behind to occupy the enemy while his comrades escaped. The Nazis flooded the streets of the city attacking with full power.

From his position on the 2nd floor of a house, Fox made an extraordinary decision. He called for an artillery strike on his own position! In a matter of minutes, hundreds of artillery rounds blanketed the area including the house where Fox was holed up. Those rounds killed hundreds of Nazi soldiers and forced the Germans to delay their advance through the town. This allowed the American soldiers time to launch a counterattack and retake the town. John Robert Fox was killed in the attack that he ordered but, by his bravery, hundreds of his fellow soldiers went home to their families after the war.

There was another man in history who made a stand as he called for an attack on his position. His name is Jesus Christ. His unparalleled act of bravery called down all the firepower of heaven on His wooden cross so you and I could live. As a result, we are part of the greatest counterattack in history! Because of one man we are positioned to take not only our city and nation but the whole world! Today, may we be like our great Commander, selflessly taking up positions while enduring the firepower of hell so that others may have eternal life!

Not About Me

This past week I was in a doctor's waiting room with several other people when I noticed an attractive woman sitting across the waiting room looking at me. I continued reading my magazine and after a few minutes looked up again and she was still looking at me. By now I'm convinced that she's not just looking, she's staring! I was beginning to feel pretty cocky until I looked over my shoulder and saw a TV screen behind me that she had been watching the whole time!

Moral of the story? Peoples' responses to you are usually not about you. Everybody you meet today is fighting a hard battle. People are hurting, stressed, distracted, and frustrated more than ever. Before you walk out your door this morning tell yourself, "It's not about me." Jesus never got offended at anybody but the religious who stayed offended at everybody!

"It's not about me" Bible verses:

"Have this mind among yourselves, which is yours in Christ Jesus, who, though he was in the form of God, did not count equality with God a thing to be grasped, but made himself nothing, taking the form of a servant, being born in the likeness of men. And being found in human form, he humbled himself by becoming obedient to the point of death, even death on a cross." (Phil. 2:5-8)

"For even Christ did not please Himself; but as it is written, "The reproaches of those who reproached You fell on Me." (Romans 15:3)

"For you know the grace of our Lord Jesus Christ, that though He was rich, yet for your sake He became poor, so that you through His poverty might become rich." (2 Cor. 8:9)

Welcome

Don't you love a great welcome? When I visit my grandkids, they run to me and hug me like they haven't seen me in a year! They make me feel like the most important person on earth! Christians above all others should be welcoming people. We were born again in Christ to welcome everyone into His kingdom. A great welcome makes others feel known, it gives them life and hope, it brings them close.

Jesus welcomed everyone—"Come to me, all of you who are weary and burdened, and I will give you rest." You can welcome someone without agreeing with their life! (Matt. 11:28) Here is what a welcoming person looks like:

1. A transformed life. We carry the amazing fruit of the Spirit! Live that! (Gal. 5:22-23)

2. Identity. When I know who I am, I can love who you are! (1 Cor. 2:3–5)

3. Wholeness. God makes our shame and our brokenness our testimony! (Galatians 2:20)

4. Purpose. The focus of God's purpose for you is permission not prohibition. That's an attitude-changer right there! (Acts 1:8)

5. Maturity. That stage of life when you discover it's not about you. (Colossians 1:9-10)

We get to welcome others—

> "For if you love those who love you, what reward do you have? Do not even the tax collectors do the same? And if you greet only your brothers, what more are you doing than others? Do not even the Gentiles do the same?" (Matthew 5:46-48)

> "When the crowds learned it, they followed him (Jesus), and he welcomed them and spoke to them of the kingdom of God and cured those who had need of healing." (Luke 9:11)

> "Therefore welcome one another as Christ has welcomed you, for the glory of God." (Romans 15:7)

What Did You Bring Into Camp?

August is a time of discovery for football players. It's a make-or-break reality that determines the course of your season, and often the course of your life. The blood and sweat have a way of finding the weakness in you. Half-hearted attitudes and selfish motivations are driven out of your system like a stomach bug on its last fling. Every time you hang up your pads after practice, it's one more opportunity stay or go, to hold on to some comfort you have fallen in love with.

And when your head hit that pillow at night, your heart demanded an answer, "What did you bring into camp! What negative attitude is in you that will negatively effect all of us? What sense of entitlement or personal ambition do you carry that will get us beat in the 4th quarter of our rival game?"

There was a time when God put a ban on certain things that, if brought into the camp of the Israelites, would kill faith and unleash compromise among His people. But the ban was broken with the result that Israel was soundly defeated by its enemy. (See Joshua 6 and 7) They were in love with their way and got blinded to God's heart.

As followers of Jesus, the only thing that can prevent us from experiencing God's grace and freedom is stuff under the ban—unforgiveness, self-pity, blame-shifting, pouting, pride, and entitlement. Don't wait til the 4th quarter of your life to deal with that stuff. Do it now so we can get the true gift of who you are! And whatever you do, don't bring it into the camp of your family, your church, or your team.

Wind Health

The biosphere is the space on the Earth's surface where land, air, and water interact with each other to support life. It ranges from heights of up to 41,000 ft. above sea level to depths of at least 26,000 ft. in the ocean. The biosphere marks the range of life on our planet.

Several years ago, scientists built a biosphere in Arizona. The idea was to create a clean, protected environment in which they planted all sorts of beautiful plants and trees. The setting was clean, but it was not healthy. Eventually the limbs of the trees began to break. The trees did not have the benefit of storm winds which cause tree limbs to gain strength!

As a servant of Jesus Christ, I often find myself praying that God will deliver me from my problems, pain, and suffering. Honestly, I want a life where everything is going my way. But that's nothing but a fake biosphere. The strength in us today is a result of God allowing us to experience the winds of adversity yesterday! Living in the middle of God's plan for our lives always gives our pain a purpose! If our eyes are on Him, we can rejoice at those storm clouds coming! The Lord "comforts us in our troubles so that we can comfort others." (2 Cor. 1:4)

What God's word says about adversity:

1. "If you faint in the day of trouble, your strength is small!" (Pro.24:10)

2. "We can rejoice, too, when we run into problems and trials, for we know that they help us develop endurance. And endurance develops strength of character, and character strengthens our confidence of salvation. And this hope will not lead to disappointment. For we know how dearly God loves us, because he has given us the Holy Spirit to fill our hearts with his love." (Romans 5:3-5)

3. "A friend loveth at all times, and a brother is born for adversity." (Proverbs 17:17)

4. "You, Lord, give true peace to those who depend on you, because they trust you." (Isaiah 26:3)

5. "I leave you peace; my peace I give you." I do not give it to you as the world does. So don't let your hearts be troubled or afraid." (John 14:27)

True

I went to high school with a girl named Jean Ann Wofford. Of all the kids in our school, she stood out as someone with a true heart. She loved the Lord and showed kindness to us, her classmates. She wasn't perfect but her long-term genuineness is a beautiful thing. When many of us were living broken and rebellious lives, Jean Ann remained true to God. I didn't want to be anywhere around her, while at the same time, I wanted to be with her all the time! I was both convicted and drawn.

A true heart is the greatest transformational force on earth. It's the reflection of an inner beauty and power that can only come through wholehearted faith in Jesus, the One with the truest heart! Here's what the He says about "true":

1. "Blessed are the pure in heart, for they shall see God." (Mathew 5:8)

2. "Finally, brothers, whatever is true, whatever is honorable, whatever is just, whatever is pure, whatever is lovely, whatever is commendable, if there is any excellence, if there is anything worthy of praise, think about these things. (Phil. 4:8)

3. "The aim of our charge is love that issues from a pure heart and a good conscience and a sincere faith." (I Tim. 1:5)

4. "And everyone who thus hopes in (Jesus) purifies himself as He is pure." (1 John 3:3)

5. "He who speaks from himself seeks his own glory; but He who is seeking the glory of the One who sent Him, He is true, and there is no unrighteousness in Him." (John 7:18)

(For many years Jean Ann Foxworth and her husband Randell served as missionaries in the jungles of Papua New Guinea. Amazing!)

Get Out in It

I'm so grateful to Rupert and Sally Buckley, my amazing parents! When we were kids, every summer we traveled to some incredible state or national treasure, camping everywhere we went! We hiked to Clingman's Dome overlooking the Great Smoky Mountains. We camped in Yellowstone National Park and the Badlands of South Dakota. We caught trout in the Pecos Wilderness Area of northern New Mexico and broiled them on a riverbank fire! We hiked to the bottom of Carlsbad Caverns, the darkest place on earth! We swam in the glacier-fed waters of Jackson Lake at Jackson Hole, Wyoming.

Those were some of the most instructive, formative times of my life! We learned how to set up and take down a camp, how to start a fire, and safely traverse a mountain trail. We learned that the world was much bigger than us and that God was truly majestic! We came to understand there were National and State Treasures we all owned together.

Get your kids or grandkids out in nature. You don't have to spend a fortune and you don't have to travel far. Our state has some beautiful state parks and dozens of hiking trails. Getting out in nature is good for the heart, soul, and body! The outdoors creates a peace like no other and a closeness to God you can't get in a building. Leave a nature legacy! America the beautiful!

The Majesty of God in Nature—

"But now ask the beasts, and let them teach you; And the birds of the heavens, and let them tell you. Or speak to the earth, and let it teach you; And let the fish of the sea declare to you.

"Who among all these does not know that the hand of the Lord has done this." (Job 12:7-10)

"For since the creation of the world His invisible attributes, His eternal power and divine nature, have been clearly seen, being understood through what has been made, so that they are without excuse." (Romans 1:20)

"Where were you when I laid the foundation of the earth? Tell Me, if you have understanding,

Who set its measurements? Since you know. Or who stretched the line on it? On what were its bases sunk? Or who laid its cornerstone..." (Job 38:4ff)

Behind the Scenes

College football equipment managers are the closest thing to the true Christian life. Seriously! Everything they do is for somebody else. On Friday they load big trucks with uniforms, shoulder pads, helmets, shoes, headsets, and footballs for about 60 players and 10 coaches. The same day they hit the road to somewhere like Gainesville, FL, nine hours and 538 miles away from somewhere like Mississippi State U.

At the stadium they unload everything, putting each player's and coach's gear in the visiting locker room, setting up the sideline with headsets, extra gear, and footballs. Their work is often frantic during the game with issues like getting a key player back on the field after equipment failure. Sometimes the game is on the equipment manager's shoulders! Yet if they get on camera, it's only by accident!

An hour after the game, with cameras flashing and autographs being signed, players and coaches are escorted to the airport for a quick trip home. The equipment managers stay behind in the smelly dressing room to load up EVERYTHING and start the long drive back to campus. For a 6:30pm Saturday game in Gainesville, FL they get back to MSU around 10:00am on Sunday. Yet they do their job every week, making everything else work for everybody else! They are the backbone!

Equipment managers represent our calling in the kingdom of God—people who are willing to do sweaty jobs unnoticed with a selfless, relentless attitude. Our job is to do whatever it takes to get everything ready for Jesus to get the spotlight! Your greatest accomplishment today might go completely unnoticed by everyone but Him! Make sure everyone around you has everything they need to succeed! Whatever it takes. When nobody is watching!

Nowhere To Go

I'm sure you've seen those homeless people out on the streets talking to nobody but themselves. I have spent much time with them and with people who knew them before they forgot who they were. This one lady, Joan, was a very beautiful woman, though the streets had robbed her brilliance. I learned that she was a successful marketing VP living beyond her willpower. Someone introduced her to fentanyl and in a matter of days she was completely overpowered by addiction. In only a few months she went from making 7 figures to shuffling down city streets! One decision. Zero warning. No safety valve. Money, pride, and DNA.

Today she had this stunned look in her eyes as if she has suddenly arrived in some strange land and couldn't find her way home. I'm so saddened by Joan's life, because she is me. I also made that one decision that ruled all others. The one that would take me over the edge of what I used to be and what I could be. The only difference in her and me was a few people who chose to enter my life in the timeliest of ways. From my own experience, here are some things you can do when you see the homeless or the poor:

1. Look them in the eye and ask them their first name. Give them a big smile, even if you don't give them anything else. To avoid them only makes you feel guilty.

2. Pray inwardly for them and ask God to break your heart over them.

3. If you're courageous enough, you might ask them how you can pray for them. Ask them if you can pray with them on the spot.

4. Offer to buy them a meal. It's probably best to go buy it yourself rather than give them the money, though I have occasionally given cash.

5. Ask them if you can hug them. Tell them you will be thinking about them and praying for them.

6. Be a part of your church's homeless ministry. (If your church doesn't have a homeless ministry or ministry to the poor maybe you can start one.)

7. Serve with homeless ministries already working in your city.

Listen to God's heart for these precious people—

"He raises the poor from the dust and lifts the needy from the ash heap; he seats them with princes and has them inherit a throne of honor. 'For the foundations of the earth are the Lord's; on them he has set the world.'" (I Samuel 2:8)

Be His hands and feet to the homeless!

SPORTS

"He gives strength to the weary, and to him who lacks might He increases power.
Though youths grow weary and tired, and vigorous young men stumble badly,
Yet those who wait for the LORD will gain new strength, they will mount up with wings like eagles, they will run and not get tired, they will walk and not become weary." (Isaiah 40:29-31)

Royal Correction

Tony Dungy was a head coach in the NFL for 13 seasons. His teams were perennial postseason contenders. He led the Indianapolis Colts to victory in Super Bowl 41. The guy could coach! When he first started working towards becoming a head coach, people wondered if he could do it. He wasn't the type to yell at players or get in their faces. Many didn't think he could control his teams. Boy did he prove them wrong!

Coach Dungy's coaching style provides a great example of the difference between correcting and criticizing. He relied on consistent motivation, first-class instruction, and timely encouragement. The rules were non-negotiable, and punishment was clear. When a player did something wrong, the goal was to help him become a better player and a better person. What is the difference in correcting and criticizing? Here are the dictionary definitions—

1. Criticize—to point out faults in a disapproving way.
2. Correct—to adjust to function accurately or in accord with a standard.

Criticizing focuses on mistakes and weaknesses while correction focuses on proper function and improvement. Criticizing often carries the components of frustration and anger. Correction is authority under control through timely and patient discipline. Whether you are a coach or a parent or an employer, if you want the best from those you lead, work toward consistent motivation, first-class instruction, and timely encouragement.

Plan To Win

Our football team had a Plan To Win—four essential things we had to get done to position ourselves for victory. Every week we preached, promoted, and lived it. The Plan To Win is amazingly accurate as a guide for faith and life as well. Check it out!

1. Play great defense. Our priority is to defend and serve our family, our coaches, and teammates (our church). ("Be devoted to one another in brotherly love; give preference to one another in honor."— Rom 12:10)

2. Win the turnover battle. Get the ball. Go get your stuff back, stuff that gets stolen by the enemy like hope, confidence, courage, and identity. Your stuff is your responsibility! Go get it back! ("Then David recovered everything that the enemy had stolen—all the women, all the children, all the sheep and camels—not one thing was missing. David brought it all back."—I Samuel 30).

3. Red zone scoring. (When we reach the other team's 20 yard line, we have to come away with points.) The team that recognizes opportunity will usually win. Don't get distracted by things you can't control and miss once-in-a-lifetime moments. ("So then let us not sleep as others do, but let us be alert and sober."—I Thess. 5:6.)

4. Special teams. Be a role player. Be willing to take the highest place or the lowest place, whichever helps your family, church, or team the most. This may be the biggest key to victory. We win only when everyone knows his assignment and completes it. ("He who is faithful in a very little thing is faithful also in much."—Luke 16:10)

Amazing how this plan can help us win in football games and in life! What is your Plan To Win?

Fan For Life

There was a season in my life after football that lasted about seven years. I had no plan, no purpose, and no place to go. During that time, I worked at several different "labor" jobs like hanging sheet rock, roofing houses, and working on a road building crew. I went from being a well-known football player to a so-called "common laborer". It was a painful experience when unkind people who knew me as a college athlete would openly mock my humble situation.

Tens of thousands of athletes will face "Life After Sport" this year. For some of them the transition will go smoothly, but many will not be able to sustain a healthy momentum. This will be true because of many reasons other than irresponsibility. If you know one such young man, you will play a role in his future. You might stand by and do nothing, or you might earnestly pray for him. You could even build a relationship with him for counsel and guidance. Or you could use your connections to get him connected to people with the resources he needs.

The number one thing these great young men need is strong, healthy relationships. What about motivating your men's group at church or surveying your community for organizations or ministries that are already working with young men. If you know of a program in your area, please share info with others. Let's get a plan now so when the season is over, we will be ready. We yelled for this kid's success on the football field, now it's time to get behind him in life after sport!

SURRENDER

"Humble yourselves under the mighty hand of God, that He may exalt you at the proper time, casting all your anxiety on Him, because He cares for you." (I Peter 5:6)

Venice Louisiana

The Atomic Power of Weakness

In March 1836, the Mexican Army under the dictator Antonio Lopez de Santa Anna attacked a rebel stronghold near San Antonio to keep Texas under Mexican domination. You know how that turned out right? I'm sure you've heard the Texas state slogan—"Don't mess with Texas!" Santa Anna wasn't fighting the right battle! Life is short. Fighting battles takes so much energy. We need to fight the right ones! Below are some examples.

You don't change anyone by making sure they say, "Christmas tree" instead of "Holiday Tree". Praying over the intercom before a football game at your high school does not transform students. Erecting the 10 Commandments carved in granite in front of your city's courthouse will never win your city to the Lord.

As followers of Jesus our weapons are not of this world but are supernaturally powerful and available only to courageous, submitted faith. Weapons like the fruit of the spirit (Galatians 5:22-26), prophetic voices of preachers and teachers, the power to heal bodies and minds, and the ability to see the greatness in others, especially non-Christians.

Jesus changed the world when He became weak, not because He was strong. "That is why, for Christ's sake, I delight in weaknesses, in insults, in hardships, in persecutions, in difficulties. For when I am weak, then I am strong." (2 Corinthians 12:10) When your humble weakness attracts God's greatness, you will become battle-ready!

Judgement—Now or Later

"Nobody ever told him the truth and now he can't hear the truth."—Strength Coach Matt Balis speaking of a former football player asked to leave the program because he couldn't get over entitlement. Ephesians 4:15 tells us to "speak the truth in love". I believe that means helping others see their brokenness while making yourself available to walk with them to wholeness. It's not a moment in time but a season in life. Don't correct someone if you aren't committed for the long haul. Coach Balis loved that player for a year before he was shown the door.

Judging others is not wrong if guided by the Holy Spirit. As followers of Jesus our only basis of judgement is His character and nature. He is just and loving. Because He is just, He demands judgment. To fail to judge someone's sin and leave them to its destruction is not loving. We must judge but we do not judge like the world does. Here's what the Bible says about judging:

1. We are called to expose darkness with light. Ephesians 5:11 says, "Do not participate in the unfruitful deeds of darkness, but instead even expose them."

2. Sometimes being silent is wrong. Ezekiel 3:18-19– "So when I say to a wicked person, 'You're about to die,' if you don't warn or instruct that wicked person that his behavior is wicked so he can live, that wicked person will die in his sin, but I'll hold you responsible for his death."

3. Many people point to Matthew 7:1 and say, "You see judging is a sin." But read in context this verse is talking about hypocritical judging. For example, how can I judge you for lying if I lie as much or more?

4. How are we to watch out for false teachers if we can't judge? (Matthew 7:15-16)

5. How are we to distinguish good from evil without judging? Hebrews 5:14–"But solid food is for the mature, for those who have their powers of discernment trained by constant practice to distinguish good from evil".

6. God's people will judge. " I Corinthians 6:2–"Or don't you know that the saints will judge the world? And if the world is judged by you, are you unworthy to judge the smallest cases?

7. Love demands that we judge but not like the world. "The person with the Spirit makes judgments about all things, but such a person is not subject to merely Human judgments." (I Cor. 2:15) Led by the Holy Spirit, righteous judgement will have the flavor of love—joy, peace, forbearance, kindness, goodness, faithfulness, gentleness, and self-control.

Every Word

I've read the Bible through a few times and parts of it many times. Yet, every time I go back to it, I see new things. A verse that I know well takes on a deeper meaning. If I take time to study a single word, I usually get something new. When that happens, I get a deeper understanding of the verses that it comes from. I like to read a whole book through over several days. Doing that I sometimes get the greater context of its words and verses that I could not have seen before. I'm gaining revelation most days not because I'm more spiritual than others but because I might be more desperate than others!

"Blessed are those who hunger and thirst for righteousness, for they shall be filled." (Matt. 5:6) That's it. You don't need a theology degree or years of Bible training. You only need to be hungry for God and He will feed you! Remember these ideas when you're reading the Bible:

1. God wants you to get it. (James 4:8)

2. Being aware of your own brokenness is what creates humility and hunger, both of which are essential in knowing God through His word. (Matt. 5:3)

3. Don't worry about what you can't understand. Run with any revelation you do get, even a tiny bit. (James 1:22)

4. Seek to know the God of the Bible and you will know the Bible of God. (John 5:39)

5. Learn from other Christians who have a track record of serving God and loving people. (Phil. 3:17)

Reading the Bible and it not the same as eating its bread and its fruit. "Man shall not live by bread alone, but every word that comes out of the mouth of God." (Matthew 4:4)

Snowflake's Chance in Hell

There is something in our country far more devastating than human patterns and systems of racism. In fact, it is the real source of systemic racism. No government will ever address it. No law can ever make it illegal. Because of it, we are all guilty, all of us—red, yellow, black, and white.

It's called systemic rebellion. Through mankind it creates and sustains hate, injustice, and suppression. For centuries ever since the Garden of Eden. All of us are born under the power of this deadly system. We as humans are the ones who have created and maintained cultures that deny God's authority and destroy people's lives.

But God, in His enduring love for us, provided an eternal solution through the free gift of His Son Jesus. In Him, systemic racism and systemic rebellion cannot be sustained. Our great hope is the simplicity and purity of devotion to Christ. If the best of your energy is not going toward doing His will and making Him known, maybe you need to stop looking for solutions and be the solution!

How about we stop fighting and start surrendering. "I can do nothing on My own initiative. As I hear, I judge; and My judgment is just, because I do not seek My own will, but the will of Him who sent Me." (Jesus, John 5:30)

New

With some of us like me who have dark pasts, if we were to mess up now, there would be people who would say "I knew it! Some things never change." If you have a dark past too, let's ban together. Let's agree to pray for one another, that we will remain strong in our new lives and that we will never go back to what we were. Let's remind one another of our new identities and who we are now! If that's you, I want you to know that I love you and God loves you and that I'm praying for you and believing in the real you, the Holy Spirit-filled you!

If you haven't met Jesus, He's standing right next to you, so why not have a conversation with Him? When we surrender to Him, our good, good Father calls us out of darkness into His beautiful light—forever! (I Peter 2:9) When that happens, we are not only saved but made pure and holy, every ounce of us, every memory in our minds! (I

John 3:3) Our Father believes in you and so do I, no matter what! How about reminding someone you know about these things today! You could change a life!

"But you are A CHOSEN RACE, A royal PRIESTHOOD, A HOLY NATION, A PEOPLE FOR *God's* OWN POSSESSION, so that you may proclaim the excellencies of Him who has called you out of darkness into His marvelous light; for you once were NOT A PEOPLE, but now you are THE PEOPLE OF GOD; you had NOT RECEIVED MERCY, but now you have RECEIVED MERCY." (I Peter 2:9-10)

"See how great a love the Father has bestowed on us, that we would be called children of God; and *such* we are. For this reason the world does not know us, because it did not know Him. Beloved, now we are children of God, and it has not appeared as yet what we will be. We know that when He appears, we will be like Him, because we will see Him just as He is. And everyone who has this hope *fixed* on Him purifies himself, just as He is pure." (I John 3:1-3)

I'm Sorry

We can be like the little kid whose parent is standing over him saying, "Tell your sister you're sorry you hit her in the head with that dirt clod!" We can get a kid to say, "I'm sorry" but that isn't the same thing as genuine remorse, is it? One of the identifying traits of a psychopath is an extraordinary lack of remorse. They can do terrifying things to people without any regret whatsoever. It's like they have this big numb place in their hearts where there is not an ounce of tenderness or compassion. Scary. I'm so callous sometimes I feel like that's me!

The definition of remorse is "deep and painful regret for wrongdoing". Remorse, or godly sorrow, is a critical part of our faith. It is not shame and it is not condemnation. It is taking 100% responsibility for our words, actions, and attitudes. God uses it to draw us back into right relationship with Him and others. Spirit-led remorse breaks the power of pride in us enabling us to be honest, to be tender toward God or people we've hurt. Remorse is a place of solace where our hearts get recalibrated in the presence of the One who knows us.

The Apostle Paul said, "I now rejoice, not that you were made sorrowful, but that you were made sorrowful to the point of repentance; for you were made sorrowful according to the will of God, so that you might not suffer loss in anything through us. For the sorrow that is according to the will of God produces a repentance without regret, leading to salvation, but the sorrow of the world produces death". (2 Corinthians 7:9-10) Wow! Let your defenses down when you have sinned. Let God break your heart with remorse so you can be wholehearted again!

THE RIVER

"He who believes in Me, as the Scripture said, 'From his innermost being will flow rivers of living water.'" (John 7:38)

Jourdan River Diamondhead Mississippi

Get Off the Bank

It's difficult to measure the power and direction of a river unless you are in it. You don't learn much from the bank, but once you get out in the water, everything changes! I've kayaked many southern rivers and streams, but none are as compelling as the Father of them all, the Mighty Mississippi! This unpredictable river is both peaceful and terrifying, comforting and unsettling. Make no mistake, it has a will of its own!

Our natural rivers and waters are a glimpse into the nature of God. Jesus said, "He who believes in Me, as the Scripture said, 'From his innermost being will flow rivers of living water.'" (John 7:37) This river-on-the-inside is the life and influence of the Holy Spirit of God. It's hard to imagine! The Creator of the universe lives in us! The one who made the river is the River, and He will not be tamed!

Religion is man's attempt to tame God, to make the river of His love and power to serve what is not beautiful and free. It will never happen. Religion will not get off the bank and surrender to the Father of waters! But you can do it! You can decide to jump in, to let go of whatever it is you think can keep you safe on the bank. If you are willing, the Holy Spirit will reveal in you those dead regulations, rules, and traditions that can't bring life. You can learn the flow of the

Holy Spirit, the freedom from religion, and the connection of your heart to God's.

"Then the (prophet) went out toward the east with a line in his hand and measured 1500 ft. And he led me through the water, water reaching the ankles. Again, he measured 1500 ft. and led me through the water, water reaching the knees. Again, he measured 1500 ft. and led me through the water, water reaching the loins. Once more he measured the same distance and it was a river that I could not ford, for the water had risen, enough water to swim in, a river that could not be forded...**It will come about that every living creature which swarms in every place where the river goes will live!**" (Ezekiel 3-5, 9)

Down To The River

My Pastor David Hale spoke to us about the Grand Canyon and the fact that over 80% of its visitors spend an average of 15 minutes at the rim. They don't camp overnight on the canyon trail or take the trek down to the Colorado River that made the canyon. They come, they look, and they return to their cars. Then, the rest of their lives they tell people about their 15 minutes on the rim! They never went deeper. They never took an adventure. They never got a close-up look at the river that made it all. 80% of them! They just got back in their cars and went back to normal.

What a powerful illustration of dead religion! We come to the edge of the River of Christ and in 15 minutes say the salvation prayer. Then for the rest of our lives we go and tell people about our 15 minutes. We never go deeper or further into the heart and purposes of the Lord. Jesus is calling you off the safe bank of your life into the wild and powerful river of His purpose! Let this season of your life be the time you get off the bank forever! The River is calling you!

Other than John 3:16, Ezekiel 47 is the most transformational part of God's word in my life. Please read, study, and meditate on this most powerful chapter!

> 1 Then he brought me back to the door of the house; and behold, water was flowing from under the threshold of the house toward the east, for the house faced east. And the water was flowing down from under, from the right side of the house, from south of the altar.
>
> 2 He brought me out by way of the north gate and led me around on the outside to the outer gate by way of the gate that faces east. And behold, water was trickling from the south side.
>
> 3 When the man went out toward the east with a line in his hand, he measured a thousand cubits, and he led me through the water, water reaching the ankles.

4 Again he measured a thousand and led me through the water, water reaching the knees. Again he measured a thousand and led me through the water, water reaching the loins.

5 Again he measured a thousand; and it was a river that I could not ford, for the water had risen, enough water to swim in, a river that could not be forded.

6 He said to me, "Son of man, have you seen this?" Then he brought me back to the bank of the river.

7 Now when I had returned, behold, on the bank of the river there were very many trees on the one side and on the other.

8 Then he said to me, "These waters go out toward the eastern region and go down into the Arabah; then they go toward the sea, being made to flow into the sea, and the waters of the sea become fresh.

9 It will come about that every living creature which swarms in every place where the river goes, will live. And there will be very many fish, for these waters go there and the others become fresh; so everything will live where the river goes.

10 And it will come about that fishermen will stand beside it; from Engedi to Eneglaim there will be a place for the spreading of nets. Their fish will be according to their kinds, like the fish of the Great Sea, very many.

11 But its swamps and marshes will not become fresh; they will be left for salt.

12 By the river on its bank, on one side and on the other, will grow all kinds of trees for food. Their leaves will not wither and their fruit will not fail. They will bear every month because their water

flows from the sanctuary, and their fruit will be for
food and their leaves for healing.

Waters

It comes and goes and steady flows,
No one tells it and who else knows
The source its path such downhill wander
From what height it moves out yonder?
Ocean speaks its message loud
And river holds its power proud.
Rain its personality
Emotions in reality.
The drop upon my fleshly cheek
What word to me does it now speak?
Could it have been the drop of blood
Shed by Him Who ruled the Flood?
The sweat upon His ancient brow
Born again in the shower just now?
While thunder sounds its power loud
And lightening deadly but so proud,
The tears of Mom who lost her child
The same that fell in the jungle wild.
Water breaks at the sound of birth
And stirs to life a bright new earth
When rivers will flow not just in beds
But in the hearts of men instead.
Healing all who drink of it
Changing who can think of it
The life of Him Who loves and heals
With supernatural grace He steals
The curse of death and makes to flow
His river in us that we too know
The same such power to serve and care
That water here that once was there.

Bill Buckley   2018

WARFARE

"Finally, be strong in the Lord and in the strength of His might. Put on the full armor of God, so that you will be able to stand firm against the schemes of the devil. For our struggle is not against flesh and blood, but against the rulers, against the powers, against the world forces of this darkness, against the spiritual forces of wickedness in the heavenly places." (Ephesians 6:10-12)

Bluff Lake Noxubee County Mississippi

The Devil Made Me Do It

Have you been taught about the kingdom of God but not about the kingdom of darkness? What do you know about Satan and his army of demons? In our culture people might laugh at you if you believe in God but want to see you locked up if you believe in Satan. Most of the "photos" we have of Jesus show Him to be a passive, frail man who wouldn't harm a flea. But He was no common civilian suffering the attacks and harassment of Satan. He was the pioneer and Captain of our salvation, the original soldier of the cross.

Satan cannot touch the finished work of Calvary, but he can prevent you and I from taking ground for the kingdom already won. It's time to take our position in "the heavenly places" beside our Commanding Officer. We are no longer free to play the role of civilians, living as if there is no war. The history of believers in every age is one of conflict. It's time we learned who the real enemy is. It's time we stopped fighting people and people groups, political agendas, and human philosophies. It's time we learned to fight the real war in the spirit realm.

Does your life express the hostility God put between Satan and Jesus? What does that look like? What does that mean for you today? Are there any ways in which you are seeking coexistence with Satan through compromise? Is your conviction about Christ and His purposes strong enough that others readily see it? My brothers and sisters, the war is on!

The Bear Truth

A guy was telling me about being attacked by a grizzly bear in Glacier National Park, Montana. He remembered being told to play dead, so that's what he did. The bear began attacking him viciously, but the guy didn't move. It soon became obvious that the bear was going to kill him whether he resisted or not! He told himself, "If I keep playing dead, I'm going to be dead!" So, he rolled over and hit the bear in the jaw as hard as he could. Amazingly, the bear backed off. The guy stood up and started shouting and running at the grizzly. The bear left, the attack was over, and the guy lived to tell about it.

Each of you have something to fight that is more dangerous than a grizzly bear. His name is Satan, and he is coming after you sometime today. You can ignore him if you want to but if you keep playing dead, you're going to be dead. He's coming to kill, steal, and destroy. You need not fear him, but you better not ignore him. Here are 5 weapons needed to fight the enemy (from James 4:5-9):

1. Humility—Pride is Satan's breath. Don't give him oxygen! Ask your spouse to evaluate your pride level.

2. Wisdom—Don't make others responsible for your fear, anxiety, and brokenness. That's between you and God.

3. Vigilance—Live ready, hour by hour, to hear and obey the Lord and you won't have time to listen to Satan. Hour by hour!

4. Relationship—Living life beside other Christians moves you from being a civilian to being part of an army! (Ecc. 4:12)

5. Identity—We fight from freedom, not for freedom! As sons and daughters of the King, we carry His authority. We bow only to Him!

WITNESS

"You will receive power when the Holy Spirit has come upon you; and you shall be My witnesses both in Jerusalem, and in all Judea and Samaria, and even to the remotest part of the earth." (Acts 1:8)

Bluff Lake Oktibbeha County Mississippi

The World Knows It's Wrong

I was talking to a woman who openly laughed at me when I told her that I was a Christian. She found it hard to believe that anyone in the 21st-century could believe in a "mythical ancient religion". But the Bible clearly states that people most assuredly do believe in a God they don't yet know. (See Romans 1) They may not openly consent to faith in Christ, but they will never convince their own hearts of what their head may be claiming. This truth gives me great confidence as I interact with non-Christians.

I told this precious woman that in her heart of hearts she knew God was real, that she couldn't fool me or herself. This truth completely silenced her. We have got to be ready for these sobering moments with unbelievers by spending time in God's presence, reading His word, and praying our days into His hands! It's our time with God that galvanizes our faith with peace and confidence so that we can share Him with boldness and compassion. "The mountains (of doubt and unbelief) melted like wax at the presence of the Lord." (Psalm 97:5–my parentheses) People are waiting for the Gospel. They just may not know it yet.

> 18 For the wrath of God is revealed from heaven against all ungodliness and unrighteousness of people who suppress the truth in unrighteousness,

19 because that which is known about God is evident within them; for God made it evident to them.

20 For since the creation of the world His invisible attributes, that is, His eternal power and divine nature, have been clearly perceived, being understood by what has been made, so that they are without excuse.

21 For even though they knew God, they did not honor Him as God or give thanks, but they became futile in their reasonings, and their senseless hearts were darkened.

22 Claiming to be wise, they became fools,

23 and they exchanged the glory of the incorruptible God for an image in the form of corruptible mankind, of birds, four-footed animals, and crawling creatures.

(Romans 1:18-23)

Radar

On the quiet Sunday morning of December 7, 1941, two Navy privates spotted something on their radar headed toward the island of Honolulu and the American Naval base at Pearl Harbor. They immediately contacted their Admiral in charge of the base. But the Commander did nothing, attributing the alarm to a couple of inexperienced rookies.

But the radar was not lying. 182 Japanese warplanes loaded with bombs were zeroing in on the naval base. In a matter of hours 2,304 Americans were killed and 6 warships were destroyed. If the Admiral had heeded the warning most of those men might have been saved.

Though I believe the Gospel of Christ to be fundamentally an invitation, it also contains the most urgent warning in the history of mankind. Speaking to those who refuse to heed the warning to repent and surrender to Christ, the Bible says, "They will suffer the punishment of eternal destruction, away from the presence of the Lord and from the glory of His might."(2 Thessalonians. 1:9)

We cannot stand by and do nothing as the enemy of our soul raids peoples' lives. We must tell them. In love we must warn them! We can do that with wisdom and conviction as we learn to be led by the Holy Spirit. Think about having a talk this week with someone you know who doesn't yet know yet that the enemy is approaching!

How To Know If You're A Christian

- You publicly say good things about people who don't like you.
- You publicly say good things about people who you don't like.

356

- You have some friends who are whatever political party you aren't.

- You don't put your trust in your church doctrines but rather in Christ.

- Your prayers are twice as long for people or groups who offend you as your negative comments about them.

- You care more about people than you do about animals or climate.

- You spend more time promoting Jesus than your own race.

- You received correction more in the last year than you gave correction.

- Your denomination is not nearly as important to you as your neighbor.

- You treat drivers and waitresses with as much respect as you do bosses and good friends.

Would you do a Bible study of these things? Galatians 5:13-26 speaks to them—

> 13 "For you were called to freedom, brethren; only do not turn your freedom into an opportunity for the flesh, but through love serve one another.
>
> 14 For the whole Law is fulfilled in one word, in the statement, "YOU SHALL LOVE YOUR NEIGHBOR AS YOURSELF."
>
> 15 But if you bite and devour one another, take care that you are not consumed by one another.
>
> 16 But I say, walk by the Spirit, and you will not carry out the desire of the flesh.

17 For the flesh sets its desire against the Spirit, and the Spirit against the flesh; for these are in opposition to one another, so that you may not do the things that you please.

18 But if you are led by the Spirit, you are not under the Law.

19 Now the deeds of the flesh are evident, which are: immorality, impurity, sensuality,

20 idolatry, sorcery, enmities, strife, jealousy, outbursts of anger, disputes, dissensions, factions,

21 envying, drunkenness, carousing, and things like these, of which I forewarn you, just as I have forewarned you, that those who practice such things will not inherit the kingdom of God.

22 But the fruit of the Spirit is love, joy, peace, patience, kindness, goodness, faithfulness,

23 gentleness, self-control; against such things there is no law.

24 Now those who belong to Christ Jesus have crucified the flesh with its passions and desires.

25 If we live by the Spirit, let us also walk by the Spirit.

26 Let us not become boastful, challenging one another, envying one another."

God is His Word! May you know Him deeply, truly, and fully!

Made in the USA
Monee, IL
19 December 2022

22936012R10197